PADLOCKS

PADLOCKS

Living with Sid and Nancy

A memoir by Den Browne

www.backstage-books.com

PRINT THE LEGEND

BACKSTAGE BOOKS

10 Cambridge Rd, Hale, Cheshire WA15 9SZ

ISBN: 978-1-7394779-1-2

Printed in Great Britain

Contents

Foreword vii

Introduction xi

1. Before 1
2. First Meeting 6
3. Evening Out With A Sex Pistol 11
4. Padlocks 17
5. The Morning After 23
6. Stranger In Blue Suede Shoes 33
7. The Uninvited 44
8. A Night At The Marquee 59
9. Autumn Days 67
10. The Tale Of Lost Lucy 78
11. Violence 83
12. Holidays In The Sun 87
13. Season Of Mellow Mists 93
14. The Autumn Cull 97
15. Winter Nights 102
16. New Year 112
17. Pindock Mews 114
18. Eton Avenue Endgame 120
19. Pindock Blues 125

Postscript – Chelsea Hotel 138

Heroin Reflections 146

A Warning from the Future 153

Some Facts and Figures 156

Sid, Nancy and Heroin 160

Thanks 169

Foreword

"Time Is the Fire in Which We Burn"

from *Calmly We Walk Thru This April Day*,
DELMORE SCHWARTZ, 1937

Why is this book different? Unlike many accounts, it's written by someone who actually knew Sid Vicious and Nancy Spungen. Although they died almost 45 years ago, a lurid industry has subsequently flourished around the ill-fated couple. Because of their infamy, Vicious and Spungen have become a grubby canvas for opportunism. Endlessly recycled, Sid and Nancy are the perfect fodder for sensationalism, the original dustbin kids, throw-a-ways, so what does one more layer of grime matter? However, there are still certain quarters where a new perspective is proffered that offers a sliver of humanity and this is one of them. I was first introduced to Den Browne by the photographer, Mel Smith, after she ran an interview with him on her webzine, Mudkiss, in which he discussed his former flat mates. What struck me most is that Den seemed to like Nancy Spungen. By acknowledging that Nancy was a difficult yet fallible young woman with some worthy qualities, he had gone against the grain, the very thing that punk promised to do but ultimately failed to deliver. The perceived notion that punk was an even playing field is sheer fantasy. Like every scene, there were insiders and vagrants. Ironically, Nancy out-punked them all. But it was the ire of the English contingent that was unparalleled.

At the time of her death, aged 20, from a single stab wound, members of the punk fraternity lined up around the block to put the boot in even further. From Johnny Rotten to Marco Pironi, no one had a single decent thing to say. I wondered if, had Nancy's death been framed differently, would this have changed people's perspectives? For example 'Girl with mental health problems brutally murdered'. While Sid Vicious continues to be revered, Nancy is perpetually condemned and yet she is his female other, albeit without a bass. Why do we consistently turn away from the fact that Nancy almost certainly was a victim of domestic violence? An industry has sprung up around 'framing' likely contenders once they've died and therefore can't defend themselves, much like Nancy on the night of her murder. Why do we find it so abhorrent to consider that Sid may really have done it? Of course he may not have intended to, but under the influence of barbiturates their last night together would have been dream-like to say the least. As this book demonstrates, violence was a factor in their relationship. Though a calamitous if likeable and at times vulnerable creature, Sid Vicious was a volatile character with a history of violence. There is no disputing that Nancy was a brat but did she really deserve such an ignominious death or to become universally derided? She had barely lived.

I tried to find the footage on-line where Nancy's mother, Deborah, finally admitting that Sid had been knocking her daughter around shortly before her demise but it was no longer available in its entirety. Scrolling through the comments posted beneath the now annotated interview, I noticed a particular statement that hadn't been challenged 'Why there (sic) always a bitch who behind rich guys? Fuck cash sucking Jews.' Yes, she was trashy and outspoken with a gratingly affected voice but why such vile rhetoric? For some sticking the knife in Nancy (who we must remember was a victim) has become a cowardly sport. She ticked all the boxes for an instant hate-figure; Jewish and overtly sexual, she arrived in the UK to greet a scene that was

largely comprised of suburban seditionaries who preferred
the symbols of taboo to direct experience. Kids who had
never left home, unlike Nancy. Or, as Caroline Coon who
knew both Sid and Nancy noted: "You are going to get a
lot of scorn poured upon a young woman who is virile, sexy
and luscious. Nancy was very confident, delicious looking.
Curly hair, blue eyes, luscious lips. I remember her running
over to say hello to me. Nancy came into a scene which was
resolutely misogynist. The British Library is knee deep in
books about the patriarchal horror of sexy women." Johnny
Rotten, who met Spungen at the same time, described her
in his autobiography *No Blacks, No Irish, No Dogs* (And No
Nancy?) as "screwed out of her tree, vile, worn and shagged
out". Can they both be talking about the same person?

It has also been suggested on numerous occasions that
evil Nancy introduced Sid Vicious to junk. In defence of his
girlfriend, Vicious told the music press that Nancy hadn't
given him anything he hadn't already tried. As the son of a
heroin user, the story has to begin and end with his mother,
Anne Beverley, who kicked him out of the house when he
was 16. Studies concur that children who grow up in drug
using environments 'normalise' the experience. Although
Nancy's background was far more affluent and conservative
than that of her beau, she was similarly banished by her
parents. Sid and Nancy were both lost children up against a
hostile world but we like polarities don't we? One hapless,
one conniving. One forgiveable, one forsaken. Real life is
never that easy…

There's not much left to say about Sid and Nancy, their
story has been rinsed until there's nothing but shadowy
projections; a snuff film on a going nowhere loop fleshing
out documentaries, articles and numerous books. Yet Den
Browne has brought something fresh to a normally tired
genre; at home with Sid and Nancy. Unbiased and articulate,
Den restores Nancy's diffident humanity and observes
Sid's unhappy metamorphosis from newly inducted Sex

Pistol to struggling solo entity. It's a brave book too, a self-confessional that might lend itself to criticism for its honesty and unflinching depiction of drug life. It also categorically debunks the notion that the UK was a narcotic free zone until big bad America arrived in 1976, charting the insidious route from supplier to street and the characters that found themselves there, the author among them.

After ten years-worth of writing in the seclusion of recovery, Den can finally look back.

Nina Antonia
September 2023

Introduction

You Can Skip This Bit If You
Just Want To Read About Famous People

This is a story about a different time in my life that
commences in the London of the late 70s, years
of heroic highs and despondent lows. While I was
hard at work screwing up my life for the next decade or so I
managed to meet some extraordinary people along the way.
No-one could ever call heroin a unifying factor, but when
I took smack with Sid Vicious and Nancy Spungen, or the
Beat writer Alex Trocchi, I felt the superior buzz of being
part of a junkie elite who'd left behind the timid straights
and their suburban concerns. That was the honeymoon
period. It wouldn't be long before it was more a matter of
protecting my stash from fellow addicts and doing all the
other bad junkie shit I'd pretended to be too good for.

Apart from a couple of older and wiser friends who
were around on the fringes of the scene back then, I'm
the only witness to most of the proceedings, and the last
one standing. There are no photos, scrapbooks or diaries
either, no mementos or keepsakes carefully preserved over
the passing years. Anything which I did have fell victim to
clearer-headed and lighter-fingered opportunists. And of
course after all this time there are bound to be mistakes of
memory and other inaccuracies. I certainly haven't got total
recall of scenes where everyone was stoned or strung out,
so allow for some poetic or narcotic licence where dialogue
is concerned.

In fact, I don't have any proof that any of Sid and
Nancy's time with me actually happened. It wasn't the kind

of thing you could document at the time – we were too busy surviving. It would have been a violation of trust and uncool to inflict "photo opportunities" on them, as their scene with us was based on privacy and being away from the Sex Pistols spotlight. I did have various bits of memorabilia – a pink and black mohair sweater from Seditionaries, a variant *Never Mind the Bollocks* in a pink and green sleeve, a signed 12 inch of 'My Way', all the singles plus a load of badges, and some prescription and methadone bottles in the name of John Ritchie. These were all stolen or lost in the free-fall years that followed. So it's all a bit Zen, a bit punk – you either believe it or you don't. Then again, perhaps you're the person who took those photos of us at the X-Ray Spex gig at The Marquee who has never come forward.

You'd also be entitled to ask why I'm writing this after so long. There are plenty of reasons. In the years after 1985 when I was rebuilding my life after getting off heroin, the last thing I felt like doing was to plunge back into the darkest waters of that time. Subsequently there were several false starts. I tried to write the story in the context of a more general punk history or traditional biography, but soon realised I didn't have the time nor the patience. At times I wondered if I even remembered enough – or wanted to – to get more than a magazine article down on paper. There was even an attempt at doing it as a graphic novel, or the time I decided to take some smack in the hope that it would re-connect me to my subject. This time there were no great highs or freed up thoughts, just throwing up for hours. I felt poisoned, and couldn't wait for it to wear off so I could get back to the world of feelings and life.

Then one day I responded to a particularly stupid post online about Sid not knowing one end of his bass from the other, and suddenly I was away; I'd found my voice and realised that the more I wrote, the more I remembered. For a long time though it was a private memoir, shared only with a few close friends when we'd read each other our works in progress. This wasn't something I wanted to go public with either while I was still doing a mainstream job. In addition I had elderly relatives who certainly wouldn't see this as something to celebrate or be proud of. Now, sad though it is that they are no longer around, I'm free to write *Padlocks* without any hindrance. Once I started writing any fears of not having enough material were soon banished. I've always had an over-retentive memory – part of me believes that we all remember everything that's ever happened in our lives somewhere, it's just a matter of accessing it – and in no time I felt like I could invoke the Eton Avenue atmosphere at will. Playing the music of the time accelerated the process. Of course I don't claim total recall where dialogue is concerned, although some of the episodes here are etched deep in me, word for word and blow for blow. I trust that I've done them both justice in trying to recreate how they talked and acted.

My life is very different now since the Sid and Nancy years, but I've tried to write in the spirit of the time and how I lived then. I trust that you'll have the sense to know that although taking drugs might be a matter of choice, things like addiction, self-harm, injecting methadone linctus, or hitting your partner with a studded belt are always a bad idea.

I've lost count of the amount of times I've been asked over the years, "So, what was Sid really like, then?" There's the view of one of the leading music writers back then (who had known Sid pre-Pistols) that he was basically an "amiable duffer" who'd been in the right place at the right time and got lucky before it all got too much for him, ending up way out of his depth in Rock Monster territory. To many now he's the first saint of punk, pure and uncompromised. Usually one of the first things I say is that he was one of the funniest people I ever knew, who could keep up a near-constant flow of sharp, witty asides, comments and insights. And, yes, at times he could be loud, crude, rude and sarcastic too – but Sid hated trivia, and generally didn't say anything, whether serious or in jest, unless he'd thought about it. But trying to recreate and convey those moments is like trying to bottle sunlight. There was a certain elusive quality to Sid, for all the full-on image, between the certainties and contradictions, which make him a hard subject to describe.

Equally, one of the most important aspects of writing this is to try to redress the balance in how Nancy has been portrayed and vilified over the years, and to move beyond the mindless labels like "Nauseating Nancy" or the marginally less offensive "Punk Yoko Ono". The more time I've spent writing and thinking about this, I realise that in many ways it was Nancy who made the stronger impression on me long-term but then that is hardly surprising given that I spent much more time with her than Sid. She was *persona non grata* in terms of Sex Pistols' activity while they were at my place, and would nearly always stay home with me and my partner when Sid was out or away. We felt that we were outsiders and misfits in common, exiled by the conformist majority. I guess there was a kind of bond established from the first moment she joyously swooped on my books. We had a lot in common, too, in our families and their obsession with achievement and display, all picked over in many a late night discussion, at last finding someone else who felt the same way. We bonded too around our addictions. In many ways Nancy saw her habit as a kind of metaphor or microcosm of the life she'd experienced up until then, the weary resignation of yet more grief to deal with. I liked to dramatise my addiction in terms of romantic and artistic rejection of a stupid and uncaring straight world. Eventually I'd realise there are much better causes to build your life on than the "Right to be a Heroin Addict", but back then we knew we'd burnt our boats and needed all the reinforcement we could give each other.

There's a fierce and sizeable faction who hate Nancy at all costs. Usually the excuses are along the lines that if she hadn't got Sid into heroin he'd still be alive now (unlikely) or simply that it was all her fault that the Pistols broke up. I made a passing mention of her online a while back, and for the next few days was bombarded with emails from an Australian punk informing me that "Nancy was a dirty shithouse whore who deserved everything she got."

"Takes one to know one," I replied – end of discussion.

On a more serious note, the general view of her has been heavily influenced by her mother Deborah Spungen's book, *And I Don't Want to Live This Life*. It's a very sensitive area, and I certainly don't want to disrespect her experiences and emotions or how she's felt since her daughter's death but equally I can't forget the intensity when Nancy would talk of her home life when growing up, being sent to analysts and therapists, then punished with medication when that didn't work. Clearly no parent wants to give their kids a bad time, but there's also a process – one I know well – where the parent becomes aware of the disapproving looks all around, and wants to shout out "It's not my fault, you know!" There's a whole industry now dedicated to medicating normal childhood/teen problems. Kids out of control? Don't worry, they aren't just Bad, they're Mad too!

Sadly, but inevitably, there's a lot of death in this story. I am the last one standing in many of the scenarios here, and I find it hard and numbing now writing about so many lives cut short. Once you get past the novice stage with junk you can't help but notice that heroin and fatalities go together like fish and chips. It's usually accidental, but not always, and all too easy to make a fatal mistake.

"Half in love with easeful death," as the Romantic poet John Keats observed in *Ode to a Grecian Urn* – and so it seemed whenever I heard of another casualty. For a long time now the only deaths I've had to deal with have been through old age or other natural causes, but then I'd feel like a junkie Ancient Mariner, condemned to seeing others going down but with no hope of personal release. For that reason the majority of names have been changed here – to spare some people's feelings and because others won't want to be reminded too much about what they were doing back then.

PADLOCKS

Before

In the summer of 1977 I was in my mid-twenties and had been living with my partner Annie for several years in a squatted garden flat in a big old Victorian house in Chalk Farm. We'd met a few years earlier, when there was still some life in the freak scene and music was mainly dominated by hippy influences, and the main drug was cannabis, with occasional dabbles in coke, speed, trips or Mandrax. Back then I'd been finishing my English Literature degree at university, while she'd been at the local poly. We'd met as part of an extended circle of like-minded friends, and soon found common interests in music and taking drugs. Living in the country outside Cambridge had been cheap and easy, but ultimately dull and restrictive. I'd been glad to get back to London in the end, by then we were typical disillusioned hippies who'd seen the Sixties psychedelic dream fade and wither and watched our friends going off to Teachers' Training College or proper mainstream careers. I'd settled for a tedious and badly paid job with some high-end booksellers uptown.

Meanwhile the counterculture heroes were disappearing into a stratosphere of super groups, solo albums, and the occasional gig or a record every few years, and there was a noticeable undercurrent of discontent about the music scene. There'd be the occasional writers like Mick Farren or Nick Kent who'd take an overview of how complacent and dull the scene had become, or it would simply be mates grumbling about how long it had been since they'd bought an album with more than a couple of good tracks.

A couple of gigs caught the mood of the times for us. I'd seen Welsh West Coast wannabes Man often over the

years, and they always put on a good show. A gig at the
Roundhouse with John Cipollina, guitarist of the legendary
Quicksilver Messenger Service, should have been a real
highlight. On the night it was dismal as the group plodded
through their set – with the star guest totally out of tune –
on a stage overloaded with hangers-on in fringed jackets
and long dresses. It all felt like a rather desperate attempt
to recreate a scene that was already on its way out. We left
early, bored by the pantomime Sixties vibe.

By contrast a solo gig by John Cale crackled with
energy and confrontation. There were a few uncertain
looks when 'Heartbreak Hotel' culminated in a white-
suited Cale writhing on the floor under his piano, ripping
a doll to pieces, howling all the while – but this was a
totally different audience to the Roundhouse crowd, in
looks, age and attitude. The Man gig had been about the
comfortable reassurance of the familiar, although we felt
alienated by the dullness of most of our friends' scenes,
the new punk movement looked like it was for a younger
crowd, much as we liked the music. These divisions have
been over-simplified with the passing of time but life is
usually more complex and nuanced than that. So instead
of the rigid border between the "Boring Old Farts", with
their "dinosaur" progressive rock, and punk, it didn't seem
strange for me to buy the Steve Miller Band's *Fly Like An
Eagle* album alongside Bowie's *Low*, or for Annie to indulge
her weakness for Genesis at the same time as buying the
'Pretty Vacant' single.

I'm not sure that we ever really thought of ourselves as
"punks". Still painfully aware of the failures of the Sixties
Dream and the hippy era, we were determined not to get
"fooled again" as The Who had put it. We weren't the only
ones feeling dissatisfied with super groups and solo albums.
One of my old Cambridge mates, Tony Wilson – of Factory
Records and Hacienda club fame – used to look us up
whenever he was off duty from Granada TV. Invariably the

first questions would be what were we listening to? "Been to any good gigs?" and "Come across anything new?" would soon follow. He'd had a brief dalliance with the early Springsteen albums, while I leant more towards reggae and conscious soul. Maybe – as my dad had predicted – I was simply growing out of this pop music thing.

So we were doing the usual when Tony called in on his way back to Manchester. We were listening to our latest buy, Patti Smith's *Horses*, as we caught up on our news and gossip. I was about to put something else on when Tony looked up and asked if he could hear it again.

And again.

Then he wouldn't leave until Annie had made him a cassette copy. It was all we heard in his car for the rest of the visit. All the same, it stopped me in my tracks a few years back reading his *Twenty Four Hour Party People* book to be credited as the person who turned him on to punk rock – with all the implications for what followed. It's a sad aside or footnote to the main story here that my friendship with Tony was one of many to be trashed as my addiction took increasing hold on my life.

Meanwhile the standard of cannabis was falling yet costing ever more. As our hair got shorter, the drugs got stronger. Coke and heroin at £20 a gram were very attractive to the weekend decadent, though the coke was generally pretty poor quality but I'd loved heroin from the start. Whatever I was doing seemed more intense and enjoyable on heroin, and if I was bored or unoccupied, it filled the gap perfectly. It also seemed to match the growing intensity of our relationship as we withdrew more and more from old friends and places. I turned Annie on to the great new buzz as part of the sharing and bonding. At first she didn't like it, drifting into strange and scary head-spaces of nightmarish Egyptian gods and shrinking doorless rooms, before spending the next day or so throwing up.

Her drug of choice was speed – my least favourite –

but after one too many wired weekends, tooth-grinding migraine comedowns and a seriously nasty eye infection brought on by all those sleepless days and nights, suddenly the deep warm total high of heroin found the opening in her life where it could infiltrate and take root. Gradually fixing replaced snorting as weekend use became daily. This is the first major boundary to cross on the way to addiction. For the first couple of years it was mainly a weekend treat, but after a while I'd started doing some before work, then at work, and so on…

One day a mate on the Camden squat scene came round. Brian was an old school hippy whose life revolved around tarot readings, massage, astrology charts and dealing hash. He explained that "some cats from Singapore" who'd brought him some of the notoriously potent Thai Sticks weed the year before were back in town. There was a problem though – this time they'd brought a load of heroin and Brian was freaked. They had no other London contacts and were understandably wary of showing their hand, but Brian told them he knew someone who might be able to help.

So it was that a few days later I met two very wary young guys in a hotel bar. A sample was provided, thus setting a course for the next couple of years. Soon Annie and I had more dope – straight from the source, too – than we knew what to do with. We could have made a fortune or just as likely, gone to jail for a long time. Inevitably the main result was both of us acquiring huge habits. To begin with I was a novice at this level, but knew plenty of fellow users, and set to marketing my wares. It wasn't long until my former suppliers were coming to buy from me. Suddenly I'd become "The Man".

But all too soon the mission was completed, and our non-using smuggler friends went back East with their winnings. I'd managed to save an ounce for ourselves, and worked out a carefully graduated month-long reduction programme. In fact it barely lasted us a week – easily done when you're using several grams a day each.

Around this time my employers finally tired of my erratic time-keeping, generally distracted air, irregularities with petty cash and expenses, and dispensed with my services. I went through the procedure of registering as an addict at the University College Hospital clinic in Camden. This meant I could legally collect a daily supply of the heroin substitute – methadone linctus – a gloopy green cough medicine lookalike. It might have kept withdrawal at bay but it was never going to be my drug of choice. Instead of the heroin high, methadone induced a blurred, dull flatness. It induced a passive, sexless mood, and I imagined that this was probably how a cat felt after being neutered. Government Drugs left a lot to be desired as far as I was concerned.

However, the Singapore Boys had promised to return in the autumn, so getting clean or staying off were never realistic prospects, whatever I said to the workers at the clinic. At least there'd been enough money for Annie to head off to her beloved Crete to detox in a place where she felt safe and away from temptation. Soon though she was scouring the island for drugs by day, and writing me desperate letters by night, "Come out here with some gear. Post me something. Anything."

The original plan had been for me to sort out a few loose ends before joining her in Crete to get well together but there was always one more thing to hold me up, more money to get, more drugs needed to keep me on course. Then the cheap morphine tablets hit the scene, the world contracted and time stopped.

Until one sunlit afternoon when I was home alone, needing a fix, when the doorbell rang...

First Meeting

I went up the stairs from the basement flat to the communal hall and opened the door. The contrast between the enclosed porch and the bright light outside made the lobby even darker than usual. I blinked to focus my eyes, then registered a spectacular shock of peroxide hair, then a more general impression of two people standing there, pale skin and black leather dominating. I recognised Sid instantly from photos in the *NME*. He stood back in the shadows, diffident behind Nancy, before speaking in a quieter voice than I'd expected, "Sorry to bother you mate, I was looking for Gerry, he said to come round, didn't say which bell…".

Nancy butted in – hearing her husky, brash New York voice took me right back there. Unlike most Brits I loved that abrasive, speedy accent except when she yelled (which would be often), "Hey sorry, we didn't mean to disturb ya".

Well, if a punk rock star and his junkette princess ringing my bell by accident wasn't outrageously cool in itself, the situation was getting more promising by the minute. Gerry was a low-level smackhead dealer who lived in one of the flats upstairs. Marooned in the pre-punk era, Gerry had a fashion sense that had stopped with The Eagles – all faded denim, feather cut hair, and aviator shades – but nothing too extreme for when he went to mingle with the leather bomber jacket boys in the pubs along the Kilburn High Road. There could only be one reason for their visiting him. However, he was notoriously 'untogether', and as he was basically a runner for a couple of other Irish dealers in the area, you'd practically get a prize if he actually had anything of his own to sell. He'd probably grovel unashamedly at having one of the Sex Pistols in his place – if he knew who they were, of course.

If you've got a habit you become adept at identifying situations that can be turned to your narcotic advantage. It's an essential skill if you are to survive any length of time as a junkie. I had a great trump card. I knew the luckless Gerry's supplier, Michael, who lived in another flat in the warren-like house. It was a gilt-edged opportunity, as long as I could gain Sid and Nancy's trust. Then I could literally go over Gerry's head and obtain a better deal – and therefore more commission for myself.

By now they'd come inside, and we stood together in the musty hall. Addicts are usually able to suss each other out on a kind of personal junk radar, so I took my chance, "I don't think he's here now, but…", they looked anxiously at each other, "if you're looking for something, I can probably help. Do you want to come in?"

They exchanged looks again. That junkie moment, that racking dilemma – *we want to score, we're getting excited at the prospect of getting high, but there's always the risk – can we trust you not to rip us off?* Equally, for my part, I was trying to show that I was one of the Righteous Guys who'd get you something good in return for a turn-on, let you have a hit at my place, and not be the bastard who'd disappear for hours, help himself liberally, then adulterate the gear to pieces, before returning with a tiny deal and tales of woe but I'd also need to be sure they weren't the sorts who'd have you running round like an errand-boy but split the moment you'd handed over the drugs.

After a moment's silent thought, Nancy spoke up, direct as ever, "So you're into junk, then?" I nodded again and then she asked, "If you can get anything, can you do it quick or is it gonna take like hours?"

"Ten minutes maximum," I replied.

Now they were smiling, "Ya sure?"

"Fucking great. What kind of gear is it?" asked Sid, having left the preliminaries to Nancy.

"Brown Persian, and there's morphine jacks there too, couple of quid each, three for a fiver," I replied.

By this time we were heading down the stairs to my flat. Once we were in the main room Nancy let out what sounded like a cry of pleasure, before dashing across the room and kneeling before the bookcase.

"Wow! You guys have *books!*" It sounded like she'd found an oasis in the desert, muttering quietly as she scanned the shelves, "hey, Malcolm Lowry … Anne Sexton … Sylvia Plath, right!" and so on, thirstily.

Soon we'd sorted out the money, Nancy counting it out carefully as Sid scrutinised the handover. I put on a jacket and went out through the back door into the garden and round to the passageway alongside the house. There was no point in putting all my cards on the table at the beginning. If they knew the main supply was in the house they'd soon bypass me just as I had done with Gerry. I climbed the outside stairs and went round to the front of the house, rang Michael's bell and re-entered the hall. I noticed his new denims – still flared – as he ushered me in. Soon I was sitting down opposite him, a smoked glass table between us covered by a loosely scattered flotsam of money, cigarette packets, drugs, ashtrays, syringes and scales.

Michael was your classic temperamental and manipulative smack dealer – with added rock star pretensions – who loved the power trip aspect of the job. Sometimes affable and generous, at others he would delight in playing teasing little games as to whether he had anything or not, especially if someone was strung out, broke or desperate. A year or two earlier we'd been good mates, as I'd put him up when he had nowhere to stay and then helped him move into the flat upstairs from mine. Drug buddies too, of course, but that gradually changed after the Malaysian Connection came about, and I was suddenly a potential rival. After that he'd often be distant or offhand with me.

Behind the fashionable trappings of his Navajo jewellery and aviator shades, Michael was still very much the Belfast home-boy, especially where women were concerned, expecting his tea on the table and for the 'wee girl' to otherwise stay in the background. In his universe, drugs were strictly for the boys. This made him very uncomfortable with Annie, who could see off most male competition when it came to drug consumption – whatever the substance – and had no time for his Victorian attitude to women. When we met he'd invariably try to wind me up about supporting her, "You'd be a rich man without that wee girl and her fuckin' habit".

Sometimes though he'd come on all concerned, "If you take my advice, tell her to stay away when she gets back. It'll be for the best…"

Since losing my legitimate income I'd had to ask Michael for tick several times. This was always risky. If you found him on his own and stoned on heroin, he'd generally be okay with it, but if you went there when he had an audience and was coked up you could easily find yourself in trouble, being mocked for the amusement of his mates and unwittingly become the night's entertainment. As time went on he'd assembled a retinue of hangers-on who'd try to make themselves indispensable and get in with The Man by laughing at all his jokes, preparing his drugs, answering the door, running errands and generally fawning. But today I could sit there confidently, and casually ask, "You okay for three grams of the brown and twenty jacks?" indicating the spread of notes in my hand before he could sneer "Got the money this time?" Michael sorted out the deal and then did his favourite trick of going into a long ramble just as he was about to hand it over. Suddenly he wanted to know all about my life since losing my job and getting registered.

"So you're on that fuckin' methadone now?"

"Yeah, it's been a couple of weeks now. I'm getting seventy mils a day."

"Well, everyone I know says that green stuff's total fucking shite. It's no good for you. You'd be better off taking the fucking gear, honest. Knock that shite on the head and throw away the fuckin' bottle, that's what I'm telling youse. And what if you have that fuckin' Annie on your back again wanting drugs all the time?"

"Look, there's someone waiting downstairs. I'd really like to stay and have a hit, but…"

I noticed Michael sway slightly in his chair as he went into a gouch – the euphoric semi-conscious post-fix state – and waved his free hand vaguely in my direction, while he tossed the gear across the table with his other hand. I turned to say goodbye at the door, but he'd already nodded out.

I closed the door to his flat and headed downstairs.

Evening Out With A Sex Pistol

I'd been gone less than the prescribed ten minutes, but when I got back Sid and Nancy had carefully made all the preparations – water, spoons and syringes spread out neatly on the table, a packet of citric acid to help dissolve the heroin and cotton wool to mop up after. Nancy had meanwhile gathered a pile of paperbacks from the bookcase, while Sid was examining our record collection, with particular regard to my box of reggae 45s. Luckily he didn't get all the way to the back of the albums and find Annie's old Genesis and ELP records (but we've all got embarrassing albums, right?). I handed over the drugs, having sorted out the half gram I'd put in for. They seemed surprised that I hadn't tried to "beat them" in any way, as Nancy put it, and gave me the rest of the gram as a turn-on, and as a kind of guarantee of future assistance the next time they needed to score. I was very pleased with how things were going. We shot up together and got nicely stoned. Fantasies of being the Pistols' Boswell or designing the first album cover drifted through my nod. The sun got lower, casting strange, beautiful shadows through the latticed windows and stained glass inlays as we reclined, smoked, talked and did more gear.

It was all very pleasant, but I knew of Sid's already fearsome reputation for wanton violence and general instability. I found this hard to equate with the guy I'd spent the afternoon with: quiet at first, but then – once he'd relaxed – amusing, intelligent and perceptive. I'd known "hard men" and self-proclaimed "nutters" in the past, who could keep up their best behaviour for a while before reverting to oafish type. Sid was nothing like that. He and Nancy were obviously crazy about each other, Young Love personified. He was very attentive to anything Nancy said or needed, and seemed far removed from the kitten-drowner of media infamy. Even when he was really stoned there was a kind of innocent, unchecked enthusiasm about him, especially when he was talking about anything to do with music or the Pistols. At times it seemed like he was afraid he'd wake up and find it all gone, and there was a real humility to his disbelief at his good fortune, allied with a determination to use his opportunity the right way. What seemed most important to him was "keeping it real", as we'd say now. Early days, for sure, and he had a lot to learn about manager Malcolm McLaren, but at last Sid was in a position to achieve everything he'd dreamt of. Now he was in Sex Pistols, and hanging out with other groups such as his ultimate heroes, The Ramones, he was in the perfect place at the right time and his honesty and clarity of vision were the essential qualities needed for the mission ahead. Together they'd bring music back to the kids with a simple, direct and cathartic connection with their audience – though maybe that's not how he'd put it himself. Sid tended to operate by deed rather than theory. At that time – between the 'God Save The Queen' and 'Holidays In The Sun' singles – the bond between Sid and "Johnny Rotten" was still strong, and for him an essential part in proving the "realness" of the Pistols compared to the fakery and opportunism of other groups.

Still being something of a Sixties romantic who used to read every word of Underground magazines like *Rolling Stone*, *Oz*, *IT* and many a music biography, I had a quaint idea that someone who was in a chart topping group, who were rarely off the front pages of the tabloid press, would be awash with money and free drugs. Over the next few months I learnt that this was not the case. The free and easy

Brotherhood of Eternal Love certainly didn't operate here. When we met, Sid and the others were on £25 a week, eventually doubling to £50 when the album came out later in the year (achieving parity with The Clash). As for the drugs, if you're a star, you'll always pay more.

That day they were flush, though, having conned "deposit money" for renting a flat from the group's management company, Glitterbest. It would become a familiar pattern as time went on, generally being their first port of call when extra funds were needed. They'd take it in turns to call manager McLaren's PA, Sophie Richmond, once they'd brainstormed a pretext for needing cash once again. By now it was starting to get dark and Nancy, saying she was hungry, asked that we all went to a burger place on Fulham Road that she liked. Suddenly Sid sprang into life, asked if he could use the phone, and I heard him say, "Yeah, taxi for John Beverley. Sure, just pick us up at 45 Eton Avenue, going to Fulham Road…"

This was the first I'd heard of the group's minicab account – available 24/7, so whatever else, we always had transport. Sometimes when Sid was too out of it, I'd have to make the call and get past the usual opening line – "If you don't mind me saying so, you don't sound like Mr Beverley…"

The cab duly arrived and we glided down from Chalk Farm and across the river. Sid and Nancy talked stoned endearments quietly in the back, almost like two small children, with the grown-ups sitting in the front. I sat by the driver, enjoying the play of lights and reflections in the growing darkness of the summer night, and thinking how utterly bizarre it was that in a few hours I'd gone from sitting at home needing a hit to sweeping across town, all expenses paid and stoned off my face, with one of the Sex Pistols. Even more absurd was how matter-of-fact the whole process had been…

And all because Nancy had rung the wrong doorbell.

Eventually we pitched up at a hamburger joint at the South Kensington end of Fulham Road, close by the Pan Bookshop and the old cinema. Sid was wearing the Teddy Boy-style red jacket with black reveres which features in many a Pistols photo, probably his black "Vive Le Rock" t-shirt, black jeans and biker boots. Nancy sported her usual boots, fishnets, cleavage and black leather, with a black beret somehow perched on the back of an exploding cascade of bleached hair. A few heads had turned as we came in, a slight buzz going round the room – "Look" and "Is it really him?" – as we were shown to a table on a kind of raised dais at the back of the place. How long till the paparazzi arrived? I imagined the captions in the morning papers, "Who is the Mystery Man Dining with the Sex Pistol?" We ordered our food, trying not to nod out too obviously, but we were in a nicely mellow mood and our burgers soon came.

We'd just started eating when I noticed an older guy approaching our table with a piece of paper in his hand. How nice, I thought, he wants an autograph for his kids. In fact he was the manager and had redress in mind. It turned out that at some point – last week to begin with, but then maybe a week or two before – some leery young punk had gone in there, tried to leave without paying, and their glass door had been broken in the ensuing fracas.

So it followed that if it was a young punk, it must be something to do with Sid, and now it was pay-back time. The piece of paper was the bill for the meal and damages. Knowing Sid's reputation for sudden violence and knowing too that Nancy had the rest of their drugs in her bag, I started to wonder if this was where the day's happy turn of events was about to be turned upside down. I could see Sid was annoyed, but so far he'd stayed calm. Later I would learn that it was alcohol and/or speed that brought out Bad Sid, smack would chill him out more often than not, which was a big part of the drug's attraction for him.

It would take me a while to realise how much this kind of shakedown – little more than a polite mugging or demand for protection money – was an everyday experience for Sid and Nancy. Apart from the occasional friendly punk (still in the minority then), they were abused, hassled and extorted nearly everywhere they went. Suddenly the manager, aware that he was getting an audience, started to demand that the bill be paid in full before we ate as much as a chip. Sid stood firm and quietly said he'd better call the police if he was so sure he was the culprit, before going on to ridicule the man's oafish assumption that if the offender was a punk, then it must be Sid.

"Look, me and my friends just want to eat in peace. If you think I smashed your door, get the law – otherwise fuck off."

I suspected that the police might not be entirely neutral in this situation, but to our surprise the man with the moustache suddenly backed down and scuttled away. Any star-struck whispers from the other diners had by then been replaced by furtive glances and seditious muttering. We finished our meal and managed to reconnect with Glitterbest transport, but I could sense that the vibe of the night was changing. Nancy was coming down quickly. She'd just about managed to keep it fairly quiet – for her – during the little scene in the burger place, but now there were a litany of moans and complaints. The euphoria of the early part of the evening was fading, and suddenly I felt a moment of doubt and insecurity. I wasn't sure of my role. Where were we going next? To a secret inner-circle gathering of the punk elite, such as it was? Or round to Malcolm McLaren's? Equally, I might have served my purpose and be sent on my way. Maybe it would all turn out to be a kind of narcotic one-night stand, a story I'd tell in future years to an increasingly disbelieving audience. My thoughts were interrupted by Nancy, leaning forward, talking as loud as if I were on the other side of the street.

"Hey Denis," she grated in a pained voice, "We still got money. If we go back to your place, can we get more?" I tried to catch her eye with a cautioning glance in the direction of the sober middle-aged driver next to me but she was oblivious. I realised she was enjoying Being a Star, even if only for a moment and only by association. For that millisecond though she ruled London. She was too much of an Elevated Being to worry about what the Little People might think of her and her drugs.

"Yeah sure," I replied as discreetly as I could manage.

Almost wordlessly our car subtly altered its position in the traffic, and we headed back through the airless summer night towards Hampstead and more heroin.

Padlocks

As we moved homeward through the traffic, Nancy's mood worsened. She was annoyed that Sid was still really stoned, nodding contentedly against her. She kept chipping away at him, trying to get some kind of reaction or attention but getting less response from him each time, apart from the occasional mumbled "Yeah right, Nance". It looked like a familiar routine for them, and was in many ways a microcosm of their relationship. Highs gave way to doubt and where Sid took things as they came, Nancy was always able to see the next sign of trouble lurking round the corner. From that start, they'd go on to abase and abuse each other until there was no further depth to sink to, and then they'd find a way back from the hate, despair and ugliness, to come together against the nothingness and start it all one more time.

Gradually her scattershot moaning – the traffic, the car, the driver – became less random and found a target, homing in on a captive and narco-tranced Sid next to her. What it came down to was that they didn't have a place of their own to live, and she'd had enough. This had an endless momentum of its own, elaborating as the night went on, involving a series of increasingly complex and vengeful tales of people on the London punk scene who'd betrayed Nancy, slinging her out of their squat to fend for herself on the street while Sid was away. She slowly worked herself up – or down, rather – into a deep well of sadness. When we stopped at some lights, the cab practically shook with her juddering sobs.

"Hey thanks Denis, you don't know what this means

to me," she said, composing herself and drying her eyes, "and Sid – I'm not going back to your mom's place, you got it?". Sid sounded ruffled, forcing an arm round her shoulders, wondering how to make it all better. Mumbled endearments didn't do it, as I heard her pull away sharply and slump into the corner of the back seat.

They'd been reduced to staying at his mother Anne's place in Dalston, crashing on a sofa in the front room. Anne lived with an old hippie boyfriend, Charlie, who passed his days eating cornflakes and smoking dope to a nostalgic Jefferson Airplane soundtrack. Sid and Nancy reserved a special contempt for the state of Charlie's pullovers, where hash burns mingled with milk stains from his cereal bowl. It was a classic recipe for conflict for so many reasons – generational, cultural, narcotic, emotional and financial. Nancy would breathlessly recount endless rows, dramas and smart put-downs as she and Anne constantly locked horns over their Sidney/John.

My own family situation was a lethal minefield of guilt trips and resentments – old and new – at the time. My relationship with my mother had always been difficult, and the way she'd instantly taken against Annie (because of her dark complexion) had increased the tension – all the same, I was surprised by the vehemence of Sid's response the first time he talked about her, "My mother's just a dirty old douchebag, and don't let anyone tell you different". He went on to relate a series of childhood stories. At times it was hard to keep up with the ever-changing places and the passing of time, but the theme was always the same. His mother's life had been dominated by drugs and having to support her habit, leaving little time for responding to a sensitive, inquisitive boy who knew when he wasn't wanted.

Time and time again he'd return to the dominating image of his childhood – his mum pushing him away so she could have a fix, resenting his presence and too wrecked to deal with him. It was a chilling image, the small child rejected for the guaranteed pleasure of her drug.

"No wonder I grew up to be a fucking junkie, eh?" he said, with a kind of derisive snort. Over the next few months I'd get used to hearing Sid say this. That first time it was with a forced laugh. Sometimes it would emerge through clenched teeth, full of anger and bitterness. At other times there'd be a kind of doomed resignation mixed with the darkest humour. I don't recall him ever talking about his father, though.

We got back to Eton Avenue and I installed them downstairs in my place while I went through the charade of "going out" to get more gear.

"Well now, you're the lucky boy today, for sure," said Michael as I presented myself for the second cash purchase of the day. A Clint Eastwood film flickered on the TV in the background, watched dutifully by the usual retinue of lackeys and customers. "Aye, stay and watch this if you like, it's a grand film".

I declined and went back downstairs, and we stayed up fixing and talking. It'd be a familiar pattern over the next few weeks. Nancy talked a lot about her family and childhood, especially her parents' materialistic consumer obsessions, absurd status games, and the constant pressure to succeed so as to reflect well on them – and as a display of gratitude, of course. As I well knew, there was a flip-side to this: do wrong – and there were so many ways to go astray, intentional or not – and you weren't only affecting your own life, you'd made them look bad, and that wasn't allowed. It was familiar territory to me, so like my own childhood, with the lack of real emotional closeness, spontaneity or honesty. A place where love was conditional and likely to be withdrawn at any moment for some small transgression against the code of the Perfect Child.

For all this madness and sadness they somehow managed to maintain an idealised and often sentimentalised view of childhood. Along with all the sex, drugs and violence around them, there was always a child-like element to Sid and Nancy – an innocent vision of childhood as the perfect time before the corruption and the compromises of the adult world kicked in. It was all summed up by the concept of "The Kids". In the same way Sid took his greatest inspiration from the youngest Pistols fans, not the punk uniform wearers or the cool London/New York fashion crowd. When we were out on the streets around Chalk Farm it'd be the young kids who'd want to come and talk, ask questions or just offer support. Sid would never turn them away, and invariably they'd leave with an autograph or a badge straight off his jacket. "The Kids" were primal, innocent but wise, with an infallible instinct to distinguish between the Real and the Fake.

Sometimes they'd revisit childhood dramas, reliving every moment of rejection and injustice. There were many tears shed (usually by him) and many raging tantrums (usually hers). Nancy could regress herself at times into her Bad Child routine, often in the form of high-maintenance dramas to do with her asthma inhaler. Beneath it all though was a simple desire to cut through the bullshit and pretences, all the unspoken rules, conventions and little social nuances of sex, class, race and money – just like punk itself, in fact – and get to something more real, more passionate, even if that meant realising that you had nothing in this big cruel random world apart from that one other person who understands and won't betray you at the first chance. How do you find love when everything and everyone around you is so fucked up you don't even know what love is? All the damaged children, where do they all come from?

Finally my eyes could stay open no longer and I knew it was time to crash out. I looked back over the extraordinary events of the day and the tiny split-second random mistake that had brought the three of us together. By then we'd just about exhausted the punk singles sounds, and we moved on to a couple of Iggy Pop albums, before I tried to make a case for John Cale's albums as crucial in punk evolution. They liked the edgy proto-punk sounds of *Slow Dazzle* but *Paris 1919* was proving a harder sell, apart from the perfect nod-out whisper of the last track, 'Antarctica Starts Here'.

As we slouched, immobile as beached fish, I considered the stoner etiquette of the situation. Even with the minicab service on call it didn't feel right to turn them out into the night – but I didn't feel like giving up my spacious bed either. In the end the dilemma was solved by Sid passing out on the single bed across the room, totally beyond waking. I realised that Nancy had been yawning pointedly, and hinting that this might be a suitable place for her to lay her frizzed and frazzled head. I indicated that I felt like crashing too, and said I'd see them in the morning.

"You sure it's okay for us to stay? That's amazing," she said in her most disingenuous little girl voice.

I nodded and went out to the kitchen, remembering that Misha the cat needed feeding, and realised that I hadn't seen her since we got back. As soon as I picked up her bowl there was a flurry of rustling in the bushes outside. Misha darted in through the cat-flap, yowling at me reproachfully as I prepared her food.

Back in the main room Nancy had given up trying to wake Sid up, and stood naked as she pushed his insensate form across the bed. I averted my eyes and slid into bed, mindful as ever of the space where Annie should be, and passed instantly into a deep sleep. I awoke hours later, sunlight streaming into the room, casting trippy patterns of lattice, light and leaves. I still felt stoned from the night before but was soon back in the routine, knowing that I had to go and pick up my methadone from the chemist. Misha meanwhile was intently dive-bombing my toes where they protruded from the duvet. I knew there'd be no peace until I'd attended to her needs. Having come to us very young, she was still not much more than a kitten, but was rapidly growing into a beautiful, sleek jet-black little cat, with her inquisitive pointed Siamese face and sharp intelligence.

As for the flat itself, there was the one large room looking out on to the back garden. To one side doors led off to the toilet and bathroom. Across the room another door led to the kitchen, where a back door led out to the garden, and stairs that led to the communal hall of the house and the front door. None of the other people in the house ever came down to the garden, and the flat had a secure, almost secret feel to it.

Someone had built a raised bed platform in one corner of the room. Annie and I had fantasised bizarre sex acts performed with one partner wedged against the ceiling, but the reality was less exciting. Climbing a ladder to bed when heavily drugged wasn't a great idea, and after Annie nearly rolled over the edge during one of her nightmares we moved our bed into the little cave-like area beneath the platform. This space was ideal for a horizontal life of getting wrecked, listening to music or watching the television at the end of the bed. Across the room was a smaller couch where Sid and Nancy now slept.

I emerged into the room and could make out the shape of their two bodies under a pile of blankets, coats and a sleeping bag. By the wall a jagged shock of black hair poked out, dwarfed by the blonde eruption alongside.

On the floor by the bed, next to the ashtray, lay two matching grey metal padlocks, their chains entwined.

The Morning After

I went out and collected my medication, and took a swig out of habit as I made my way back up the hill to Eton Avenue. Not that I needed it after the previous night's session. Sid and Nancy were up and dressed when I got back, smoking listlessly. I made coffee and was amazed to find that Nancy took even more sugar than Annie. We had a hit, but just as I was relaxing into the warm flow of the buzz, Nancy started talking, picking up pretty much where she'd left off in the taxi the night before. If it wasn't for the difference in volume you'd call this a "stage whisper" – it might have been addressed to Sid but was really intended for me.

"Hey Sid, we gotta go back to your fuckin' mom's now?" she asked, her voice a mixture of resignation and irritation. Before he could reply, she continued, gathering momentum, "So when the fuck are you gonna tell Malcolm we need a place to live? Steve's getting a fucking huge motorbike bought for him for Chrissakes. John's getting a goddamn house. He's gotta give you the money for a fucking flat – but you keep putting it off…" Next she was mimicking him, pushing her face close to his – "Oh I forgot Nance – I'll do it tomorrow Nance…"

Sid mumbled vaguely without looking up. Sometimes there is a lifetime "between thought and expression" – as Lou Reed observed – but at others there's only a split second. It seemed the natural thing to do, so I said, "Well, you can stay here for a while till you get somewhere. There isn't much room, but…" but – there'd be a ready doorstep supply of drugs here. I can't pretend my offer was totally altruistic or spontaneous, or that I was unaware of the potential advantages of the situation.

Nancy's face lit up and suddenly she was infused with purpose and energy, goading Sid into action and then calling the taxi. A couple of trips between Chalk Farm and Dalston later, and they were installed at my place. Bags and bin-liners full of clothes, records and of course Sid's immaculate humping great new white Fender bass.

The next few days passed in a cheerily opiated haze as they settled in. Much time was spent checking out each other's records. Towering over everything else for Sid was the first Ramones' album. I'd always thought they were okay when I heard them on *The John Peel Show*, and loved the way they'd mangled Sixties surf music and teen pop with contemporary urban stress, all done with incredible economy and a classic pop sensibility. Now I had the chance to really hear it at close quarters I was awestruck by how much was going on in the lyrics and music. Superficially The Ramones could sound very basic and repetitive, but on repeated listening the songs would open out and expand like notes from a sketchbook, all bursting with hooks, changes and ideas. In addition, Nancy was able to provide a full commentary and scene-setting for most of the songs – so I was in no doubt as to what went on at 53rd and 3rd, or why Dee Dee had to be there. Like Bowie at his peak (another Sid favourite), the ideas came at such a pace that there was only time to lay out some guidelines for future use and then move on. We both had the Lenny Kaye *Nuggets* compilation of Sixties proto-punk bands, and that got played as much as anything else. Otherwise lots of New York Dolls and Blondie, *Marquee Moon* of course, some Jonathan Richman and The Modern Lovers, while Iggy – solo and with the Stooges – provided common ground, along with some older sounds like Alice Cooper and Lou Reed solo albums.

At last I'd found someone who didn't hate every second of *Berlin* and they'd listen intently while I told them about the show we'd seen him at the Rainbow on the *Rock 'n' roll Animal* tour, where Annie had tried to grab Lou Reed's syringe when he threw it into the audience after pretending to shoot up on stage. There were also some things I didn't like. I never saw the appeal of The Runaways, while they didn't seem to share my enthusiasm for Patti Smith. Sitting nearest the stereo I was DJ by default, mixing it up with Bowie, Stooges, Velvet Underground and some roots and dub seasoning.

It was a nice enough interlude, but there'd soon be more pressing matters for all of us to deal with. I was having a rare evening to myself when Annie's mother rang. She was a lovely lady, and to this day one of the best cooks I've ever come across, but her heavy Italian accent could be hard to follow once she'd got going. She was tangling her words up even more than usual, but one thing was very clear – at last Annie was on her way back from Crete. "Maybe she come here to Brighton first, no?" she continued, "Her papa want to see her too, she been away so long." Her dad was great too – as old school English as her mum was the full-deal Italian – though of course these loving and welcoming parents had no idea of the battle between the narcotic and erotic that defined our relationship.

My mind practically incinerated at the thought of her coming back and the realisation of how much I'd missed her. But love and desire were soon undermined by other intrusive thoughts, unwelcome but unavoidable. Had she finally managed to get off her habit? Did she expect me to have come off too?

I doubted it.

It already seemed like ages past, but it had all happened that year. When our Singapore-assisted intake had peaked earlier that spring and money was still abundant, we'd made our plan for her to head out to Crete. She'd spent time there before, and knew the coolest, cheapest places to go. All she had to do was set things up and I'd go out to join her for the sea and sun healing treatment. Of course it didn't turn out that way. The departure of the smugglers – albeit temporarily – simply left a gap for the likes of Michael to fill, and there always seemed to be something else to do before I made that trip to the travel agents. Meanwhile Annie was finding that the psychedelic international backpacker venue of previous years was now the holiday destination of choice for half the coke dealers in Amsterdam. In addition she'd managed to attract the attention of Cassie, a paranoid and manipulative New Yorker, who constantly tried to fill her head with dangers that only she could prevent.

It was frustrating that I had no means of contacting her, but her first postcards home were positive – everything was great apart from me not being there, and why would you want to knock yourself out with heroin when you were surrounded by cool people and natural beauty. These soon gave way to longer, rambling airmail letters, sometimes angry with me for still being in London, sometimes passive, remote and downbeat. It wasn't long until naked need burst through, and the envelopes contained just torn scraps of paper, "Come now, you've got to bring me something or I'll go crazy." One particularly desperate SOS got sent to my mum's address by mistake, to be seized on triumphantly as proof of Annie's unworthiness.

Above all, how would I tell her about my new house-mates when I knew I should be providing a safe place to come back to? Having Sid and Nancy there might indicate that things weren't stuck in the same place as before, but it was hardly ideal for our reconnection and rediscovery after months apart.

She rang a couple of days later to tell me she was staying with Andrea – a sour-faced humourless teacher – at her place in Highgate. Andrea's best mate was Ella, an old friend of Annie's who'd always loathed me, so I could see what was happening. She sounded wary and uncertain. For my part, I could see how she felt torn between me and her friends, but I wasn't comfortable with feeling that she was under permanent scrutiny from them. She said she wanted nothing more than to see me again, but was terrified of getting back into smack. After a while I realised she wasn't even going to ask if I'd got off, it was that obvious that nothing had changed. I explained that I'd got registered, so that things were more stable with my methadone prescription, but admitted I was still doing heroin "occasionally."

"Yeah, I'd worked that out," she said wearily.

Having got that far it was best to tell her the rest. I had no idea if I'd be playing my ace of trumps or driving her away for good. I tried to sound casual as I began, "there is something else. There's a couple of people staying here for a bit. Remember the Sex Pistols? Well, I met Sid Vicious and his girlfriend. They haven't got a place to stay, so they're living here…"

When Annie had left Glen Matlock had still been in the group, with Sid a mere footnote for people to name-drop when writing about the Pistols' entourage. However, word of this news had duly reached Crete like the echo of some distant volcano. I reassured her that the "Vicious" name was ironic, but mainly I was surprised at the lack of reaction from her. I promised we'd have the place to ourselves when she came over the next day. She insisted that I wasn't to do any drugs in her presence or offer any temptation, before adding that she couldn't promise that she'd stay either. I felt this was probably more for the eavesdropping Andrea's benefit than mine.

I wasn't sure how it would go down when I explained the situation to the others. I'd mentioned my girlfriend detoxing in Crete a few times before, but there were always more immediate things to deal with. I needn't have worried. A couple of Nancy's New York girlfriends had turned up in London and were now part of the Heartbreakers' extended family, and she was eager to see them, turning up triumphantly with Sid on her arm.

We'd arranged to meet first in Camden. I was relieved when Annie turned up unaccompanied. I'd expected Ella or Andrea to be on guard duty. I'd limited myself to a small dose of methadone that morning as I wanted to be clear-headed for the occasion, and didn't want to torment her by turning up stoned. We hugged in silence. She was back to looking like an Italian version of Chrissie Hynde, with her black hair supercharged by the Mediterranean sun, radiating subtle hints of colour and she was more tanned than ever, the junk squat grey pallor banished at last.

Soon though we were all over each other, so much to talk about, so much lost time to recover. For a few moments I think we believed that we could have a relationship that wasn't poisoned by drugs and we could prove all our detractors wrong. A few hours later I was lying back in bed, watching the smoke from Annie's fag curling upwards. She pulled close to me, resting her head on my chest for a moment, then looked up and made eye contact, "So when are we going to have a hit, then? Don't tell me you haven't got anything. I can tell you've had something today…"

I'd anticipated this moment so many times in the previous weeks, wondering what I'd do, and rehearsing different replies. I knew I sounded insincere and unconvincing as I tried to put her off. What would be the point of going back to how we'd been earlier in the year?

"We don't have to be stoned to have a good time, you know," I started, faltering as I realised how fake it sounded.

She snorted derisively as she turned away from me. Technically she was clean, but only through force of circumstance. I knew how merciless the craving could be – much worse than the physical effects of withdrawal – and how unrelentingly it would nag away until finally you'd succumb just to stop that endless argument in your head. And so in the end I gave way, in order that we might return to familiar territory, with me back in the Big Provider role.

We turned on together, and once again I heard her say,

"Oh Denis that feels so good."

Of course, that only postponed the really serious issues. Annie knew that she'd broken her curfew by staying over and feared being grounded by Ella and Andrea, especially if she went home stoned. I could tell she was still uncertain about coming back – to me, the drugs, London, everything. One moment she was sure that yes, it could just be an occasional treat, the main thing was our relationship. Soon though the guilt would return – why had she succumbed so readily to temptation? Why hadn't I told her no? Gradually this unspoken undercurrent undermined the happy vibe of being together again. I could feel her eyes following me every time I moved round the flat, hoping that I was getting something for her, and making sure I didn't slip off for a discreet hit on my own.

"Well, I might as well be off then," she announced, breaking the silence, before skewering me with the question I'd been dreading, "Can I have something to take back with me?" This broke it all down to its simplest formulation. We love each other. But we both love heroin even more.

Could we ever resolve this triad?

In the end I sorted her out a small bag, but warned her to be cool with it, preferably not to shoot up, and to generally make sure she didn't give Ella and Andrea easy ammunition to use against us. I was marked down for all time as the Evil Lothario who'd corrupted her with brain-bending drugs and destroyed her will to resist my wiles. Never mind that it was "consenting adults" all the way.

For a moment I remembered when we were first together several years earlier when she was living in the country; staying up all night talking, driving out to watch sunrise on the Downs. After a while she'd asked me to include a little packet of this or that when I wrote to her during the week. It seemed so innocent compared to now.

"Look, just do a little line when the others aren't around. Don't get too out of it. Remember – you haven't got the same tolerance now. Just enjoy it sometimes without getting a habit." She didn't take her eyes off the packet in my hand until I'd handed it over.

She was back a couple of days later, grey-faced and retching as she reached for me anxiously. She pressed her head to my chest and moaned, "For fuck's sake Denis, get me some gear, I'm feeling really sick". I've never really bought into the "Instant Addiction" idea: one hit and you're hooked for life… The vast majority of people who've tried heroin don't turn into addicts. Early heroin experiences usually involve a lot of throwing up, which is enough to deter the majority. It does actually require a certain commitment to acquire a habit. But such are the perversities of addiction, that it can come racing back unbidden if it senses fertile ground or a moment of weakness.

I felt for Annie in her distress, but couldn't understand how she'd fallen so far so quickly. She explained that she'd gone straight back into junkie mode on autopilot, carefully measuring her supply out into fixes, starting with that fatal leaning-out-of-bed hit in the morning after she'd heard Andrea leave for work. I'd wanted to be sympathetic and loving, but now I was angry, and – to my surprise – even a little shocked.

"You're un-fucking-real, Annie – you'd got off your habit. I gave you that gear so you could have a little buzz at the weekend or the odd bedtime line. Not to start acting like you're strung out again already. You know what'll happen if you start hitting up the moment you're awake. It just seems like you're still clinging to it. Are you afraid or something?"

"That's almost funny, coming from you," she snapped angrily, then – before I could reply – switching to her most soulful one-to-one voice. "I thought you understood, but maybe you don't. I was sick so fucking long. It never stopped the whole time in Crete. But I always thought of you…"

I knew I'd been too judgemental, and it was hardly as if I was preaching from a position of strength. Sure, I'd been sick and strung-out enough times but never for that long. In a couple of years' time I'd know all about the aching craving that would never leave me alone. Sometimes I'd think I was doing alright and keeping away from the dope, but the lurking urge would bide its time, then surge back, taunting me – did I really think I'd win that easily?

Seconds, minutes, hours, days, nights, weeks, months, years – each one had to be fought through. All the time I had no energy, hardly any sleep, my mind narrowed down to monochrome, thinking of all the possible meanings of "out of it" from the blissful highs to the exclusion and isolation. Eventually, like Annie, you'd weaken just to stop the whole damned merry-go-round in your head, reasoning distorted by need, until the idea of surrender seemed the only way of banishing the incessant voices mocking your weary soul. Taking some heroin again at least got the wretched battle over with … if only to set up the next one.

For a couple of days she wavered, physically and mentally, between returning or staying with Ella or Andrea. Then, one day, she stood there with her guitar and her usual paraphernalia of clothes, paperbacks and notebooks, and I knew she was back. She'd also been back to her old clinic at St Mary's hospital in Paddington. There she'd been welcomed like some long lost family member and fast-tracked back on to her old methadone script with barely a question asked.

Like me, she felt that the fortuitous meeting with Sid and Nancy was a kind of omen that our situation and prospects couldn't be entirely negative if we were moving in the orbit of the most happening band of the moment. It might not be the worst time to get in early with a potentially mega-rich pop star either. Maybe there was a way this could all work?

As I'd expected she and Nancy hit it off immediately. When Annie was up and on form, she was the smartest, wittiest, deepest woman I'd known. But when she got down she'd get hopelessly depressed, bitter and loathing everything and everyone, especially herself. Like Nancy she had a ferocious temper, but where Nancy's explosions tended to follow a slow-burn pattern, Annie's moods would come like a sudden storm on a placid lake. Nancy's in-yer-face energy and carefree "don't give a fuck" attitude (as long as her needs were catered for) lifted Annie's spirits. It was good to see her with a new friend, and for once a female friend who was a partner in crime rather than an adversary. For her part, Nancy loved Annie's spontaneous cool vibe and subtle, refined humour. They'd pore over Annie's scrapbooks intently, the silence broken only by the occasional remark from Nancy.

"So you're into Anaïs Nin too, then?"

Stranger In Blue Suede Shoes

It begins with a blessing
And it ends with a curse
Making life easy,
By making it worse;
My mask is my Master,
The trumpeter weeps,
But his voice is so weak,
As he speaks from his sleep, saying
Why, why, why, why are we sleeping?

'WHY ARE WE SLEEPING' BY SOFT MACHINE

Sundays are a bad day to be an addict. Back in the 70s it still meant an almost 1950s like total shutdown of shops and services. Everything was that bit more difficult and took longer. And if you were on the wrong side of the law, there were far fewer opportunities for hustling or raising cash, plus you were much more visible. If you were registered you'd get a double dose of methadone for the weekend, but somehow this always seemed to come up short, and anyway, two days of nothing but the green linctus was a pretty dull prospect. In addition, many dealers stipulated that Sunday was their day off. So even if you had money, you could easily find yourself "all dressed up with nowhere to go." But pestering The Man – however strung out you were – was a bad move that could have serious repercussions if favours were needed in the future.

Annie and I had picked up at the chemist's on Saturday as usual. Sid and Nancy were in a listless, whiny mood when we got back. We ended up giving them enough of the green gloop to get them straight – "Hey we'll score later and sort you guys out then," promised Nancy. It soon turned out that we actually only had a tenner or so between us. Still, we could use that as a start in getting some tick from Michael. Annie went upstairs, while Sid and Nancy suddenly burst into life, tidying up and once again fetching all the injecting accessories in readiness for her return. I noticed them exchange eager glances as we heard the top door open and close as Annie came back downstairs. I knew straight away from her grey face that it wasn't good news.

"He hasn't got anything," she said. This was about as likely as *The Sun* not having a Page Three girl.

Sid swore quietly. Nancy flared, "Like fuck he hasn't! Can't you go up Denis?"

Before I could answer, Annie continued, "Well, he did look a bit sick actually and there's a couple of people waiting there. He says there should be something later. He'll let us know, but it'll be strictly cash…"

We quietly absorbed the implications – good and bad – until Nancy remembered that someone had dropped a couple of the morphine pills on the floor recently. At the time we'd been too out of it to bother looking for them. Suddenly a frantic feral finders-keepers search started – we practically fought each other to be the first to look under tables, beds or chairs. As if the two little pills were going to do anything for the four of us. They were never found, but the episode generated a lingering mix of paranoia and suspicion – what if someone had got lucky, but decided to keep quiet?

The next morning – strung-out Sunday – I could feel Nancy's eyes on me as soon as I awoke.

"Hey Denis, you want a coffee?" she asked quietly, eager to please. I nodded and felt under the mattress for the remaining methadone when she went out to the kitchen. There was barely enough left for Annie and I, let alone anyone else. Annie was still asleep. For a moment I felt the horrible demonic temptation surge, "Hey, why not take it all yourself? You'd be okay then," fighting it down as I glugged my half from the bottle with one hand and nudged her awake with the other. I passed her the little bottle wordlessly and watched as she gulped it down, also silently, before leaning out of bed for a cigarette.

Nancy came back with my coffee, "Hey Annie ya shoulda called out. I'd have made you one too."

She lit a cigarette as Annie moved across to let her perch on the edge of the bed. We all knew what was coming next. I could see past Nancy to where Sid was tossing and turning restlessly in bed on the other side of the room. "I'm not too bad," she started, bravely, "but Sidney's getting pretty sick. Can you guys help him out with some methadone till later? That'd be fuckin' amazing…"

Once again there was no need for words. I held up the empty bottle for her inspection.

"Is that it? You coulda saved some…"

With that she snatched the bottle from me, tipping it up vertically in the hope that some homeopathic trace of linctus might miraculously appear and rescue her.

"Oi! Nance!" Sid was now officially awake and was not pleased. The first thing he'd seen on raising his head was Nancy putting down the very empty methadone bottle. She quickly made her way back across the room to reassure him before his mood got any worse. She leant over and half-whispered, "I tried to get you some. They'd already taken it. Fuck's sake, I haven't had any either, I'm sick too". I heard Sid mutter something about "selfish bastards" but typically the majority of his anger was reserved for her.

"Fucking useless. You couldn't even get a bit of methadone. Fucking chippie weekender" – this was a particularly potent insult between them, meaning someone who only dabbled in hard drugs – "You'd be back in the fucking gutter if I didn't take care of you. Dunno why I bother".

This was usually the prologue to a serious argument or fight, but he didn't seem to have the energy to pursue it this time, or was just resigned to the situation.

Meanwhile Annie tried to pacify things – "Anyone want another coffee?" – as she made her way to the kitchen.

As you might have gathered by now, it's an endless and unwinnable war of attrition being a junkie, but sometimes the angels do seem to be on your side, if only for a moment, directing light to where it's needed.

When she returned, coffees in hand, she glanced round at the others – now briefly at peace – before giving me a conspiratorial smile. To my surprise she suddenly darted her hand down the front of her pants, quietly pulling several tightly folded £20 notes. Climbing back into bed, she explained, whispering in my ear. While she was out in the kitchen waiting for the kettle to boil, she'd had a sudden flashback. On the wall there was a black and white photo from a magazine – a typical French country scene, straight dusty road through fields with tall trees either side – fixed to the wall with glue at the corners. Suddenly she knew there was something else about that picture and quickly reached out her hand, deftly running it over the trees and fields. Yes – there was a slight change in contour in the middle…

The previous summer, when we'd been awash with drugs and money it had got to be a problem where to simply keep everything safe. One Sunday night we came back from Brighton to find the lock on our front door sawn through. The would-be robber hadn't found what he was after – we had most of it with us – but it was a warning. When I changed my trousers I'd find a roll of notes in the pocket more often than not, or I'd be reading a book only for a packet of gear to fall out. Annie could be fanatical and devious about such things, so one day when I was out at work she'd spent the afternoon hiding money behind the photo and meticulously pressing it flat again. After that she'd probably forgotten about it. I could have cried as she

showed me the cash. So many times later that summer –
after the drugs and money had run out – I'd spent hellish
strung-out nights ransacking the place in the hope of
finding some forgotten stash of dope or cash and all the
time salvation had been hiding in the kitchen.

As Lou Reed so memorably observed, "First thing you
learn is you always gotta wait," and there was still another
hour or so until Michael would be available for business
– always assuming he'd restocked after yesterday's knock-
back. I could feel the first twinges of withdrawal when I
eventually made my way up the stairs. I made sure I could
hear voices before knocking quietly on the door. Michael
could be temperamental and was liable to take offence at
real or imagined transgressions of his rules or any lack of
respect, such as turning up too early. Evidently he'd got
fresh supplies and had his first hit of the day, as he looked
dazed and unshaven when he opened the door.

"Ah, right on time, eh? You'll still be wanting some
tick I suppose? Oh, I'm too generous when you boys come
taking the bread off my table."

A nasal female voice called out from behind him, "Tell
them cash only, Michael."

This was Mary, Michael's girlfriend from Belfast. When
she'd first arrived, she'd been ill-at-ease and out of place
in her boyfriend's dealing scene, fussily picking her way
among the slumped bodies, tidying up, emptying ashtrays
and generally trying to be the little home-maker. But it
wasn't long till she succumbed, and now she had a habit
too, and with it a vested interest in how the business was
run.

She still looked like one of Bucks Fizz though, even
when she nodded out over her cigarette. "You're after
burning the house down, for fuck's sake!" Michael would
snap as he shook her awake.

I could tell he was about to start the usual cat and
mouse game over credit, so I forestalled him by silently

pulling the miraculous money out of my pocket.

"Can you do us a couple?" I drawled as casually as I could.

His surprise was evident, and his tone changed abruptly. Suddenly we were mates again, chatting away as he weighed out a couple of grams. I thought I'd take a hit in the relative peace there before returning to the strung-out waiting-room downstairs. I was just relaxing into my buzz when the doorbell started ringing insistently.

Michael pulled out of his nod, and snapped at Mary to get the door. Now I was briefly one of the blessed, the inner circle who'd paid for their gear and were allowed to hit up and hang out with The Man. There'd always be something amusing in the comings and goings of the endless narcotic soap opera. I was jolted out of my reverie as Michael spoke, with evident displeasure, "Oh, it's you Gael".

Sure enough, it was one of the less welcome members of the local smack scene, Gael, a notorious rip-off artist. She had a radar for detecting and attracting strung-out addicts who – for one reason or another – were unable to score for themselves. She could always sniff out something, somewhere at times of crisis. Just trust her and everything would be okay, would be the spiel. She'd only want a little turn-on as payment. As always she was wearing her floor-length red hooded dress which, combined with her lank straight long hair, gave her the look of an aspiring member of the Manson family.

She'd ripped me off the year before, disappearing for hours, returning with eyes pinned and voice slurred, acting like she'd done me some huge favour as she handed over a pathetically small wrap of heavily cut gear. As the writer Alex Trocchi observed, there are some people who get junkies a bad name, and she was one such. Now she was trying to avoid eye-contact with me, using her hair as a convenient curtain. Eventually I managed to catch her eye long enough to direct a serious scowl in her direction.

She came to a bad and violent end a few years later when she tried her disappearing trick with the wrong people, but that's another story.

Now she was giving Michael her latest tale and trying to ingratiate herself. He was well aware of her reputation and was stonewalling her. All went well until he asked how much she was after, and did she have the money for it. Gael replied that, well, in fact it was for a friend of hers who she'd left waiting outside.

"Oh the dear God! I might as well put up a sign, Get Your Fuckin' Drugs here," Michael snorted derisively.

"I didn't want to bring him in. But he's totally cool. He's a really nice guy," then, warming to her subject, she smiled as she continued, "actually he's a rock star – you know, he's come over here and run out of gear. He doesn't live in London any more so he doesn't know anywhere to score." The mystery man clearly had the sense not to hand his money over to Gael upfront. Michael looked intrigued at the mention of a rock star – although this could just as likely mean another defiant punk like Sid as one of The Eagles making an unlikely crash landing in Hampstead. He nodded wearily when Gael asked if it was okay for her to bring her mate in.

"You know she's trouble. Why didn't you send her away?" asked Mary, briefly stirring from her nod. Michael ignored this intrusion into his business, but turned to me and said, "You keep a fucking tight eye on that girl, she'll be looking for something to steal."

When Gael returned she was followed by a tallish man with a stooping gait wearing a nondescript dark jacket and tight faded jeans. Longish sun-bleached hair framed a lean and sun-tanned face, which now bore a strained expression, enhanced by the stubble and watery eyes. He had the air of some exotic bird blown off its usual migratory course and now found itself cast down in a strange and cold place. He seemed ill-at-ease as he looked round, uncertain whether it was alright to sit down, or whether he should wait for a cue from Gael. And there was indeed something familiar about him. Suddenly I knew … my mind swirled back to the late Sixties free concerts in Hyde Park, earnestly studied album covers, *Shooting at the Moon*, Robert Graves and the White Goddess… The Stranger in Blue Suede Shoes.

How bizarre. Kevin Ayers. I'd never expected to meet one of Soft Machine anyway, even less under these circumstances.

As he was doing his business with Michael, Gael hovered like a hawk while the brown powder was dispensed. Having missed out on the cash, she wasn't going to let the gear escape her. Just as the visitor was asking politely if it was cool to get straight there, the door buzzer went again. More business. Having completed the transaction, Michael was losing patience with the throng in the room and all their differing needs.

"No, I'm sorry man, it's too busy here. In fact youse can all go now."

Gael could see the situation slipping away from her. First she suggested she was due something from Michael for bringing him some custom, but no luck there. So she turned her attention to her friend, demanding that he give her a turn-on. I'd just started talking to Kevin when she butted in. It was one of those perfect open-goal moments that life occasionally presents you. I bided my time, before casually saying, "You heard the man, Gael. Unless you've got my money from last time you can piss off!"

She snarled briefly before Michael hustled her out of the door as he went to let in the next wave of customers. I turned back to Gael's intended prey, "It's okay, man, you can have a hit in my place downstairs."

When we got back down the air was thick with expectation. Annie looked up nervously, "You were ages. Has he got anything?" Nancy was ahead of the game as usual, and had spotted instantly that I'd had something,

"Hey, nice – we been getting sick while you're turning on upstairs," she snapped.

I put some of the gear down by the waiting spoon and water, immediately lightening the atmosphere. "Oh, this is Kevin by the way. He's come down for a hit, he's okay".

Everyone else was so intent on preparing their fixes that no-one paid any attention. I made sure our guest had what he needed and decided I'd definitely earned another turn-on. As always the tension dissipated as the drugs were ingested and for a brief passing moment the place was suffused with a benign atmosphere as rushes took effect and troubles evaporated.

"That's really nice gear, man," said Kevin as he stood up, slightly unsteady. He then walked over to where Sid and Nancy were sitting on their bed, extending his hand in friendship, "Hi man, my name's Kevin…"

Sid looked up from his gouch, gave him one of his lopsided squinty looks, and managed a nod in return. He repeated his introduction to Nancy, who yawned, "Yeah, I heard yah the first time."

It was clear that he had no idea who they were. He rejoined Annie and I, slightly nonplussed. Immediately Nancy turned to Sid, and put on her Exaggerated Stage Whisper voice when she spoke, "Fuck, who's that old HIPPY guy Den's brought down?"

This was the kind of stoned banter they loved and excelled at, gently egging each other on, Sid playing it deadpan while she fed him his lines. Fortunately Kevin was too stoned to take much notice as Sid gathered momentum, "Hey ma-an, let's eat cornflakes and listen to Jefferson Airplane…"

Funnily enough, they could have had a conversation comparing notes on life in Majorca, Kevin's current abode and where Sid had spent some of his childhood with his mother. However, there was no way this connection would ever be made. Most of the time Sid and Nancy's irreverence and disdain for established values was funny and refreshing, but at times it could tip over into a childish desire to shock, trying a bit too hard to top each other in offensiveness – like their game, "Spot the Nigger", a favourite for shocking the straights on the bus. Any passing Black guys would be appraised at maximum volume and awarded points in various categories like Soul Boy, Rastaman, Afro Dude and so on. This afternoon was starting to go the same way.

Kevin had spotted Sid's white Fender bass and Annie's acoustic guitar propped against the wall, and moved towards them, asking if I was a musician too. Before I could reply Sid snapped, "Oi! That's mine. No-one else touches it, okay?" (conveniently forgetting the times it had been used as collateral with Michael). Annie noticed Kevin's crestfallen expression and offered him her guitar. He sat down with a languid smile as he carefully tuned the guitar, to a background of whispers and sniggers from the other side of the room. Eventually he started to play, a rambling flamenco gradually giving way to a slower, Miles Davis-like melody which he hummed along to, head bent forward intently. When he finished, Sid snorted, "Oh wow man, I wish I could play like that!".

The sarcasm was obvious and unpleasant. Kevin quietly assembled his things, stashed his gear, ignoring Nancy's cheeky request for a turn-on, thanked me for my hospitality and was soon away into the wintry afternoon.

Inwardly I was seething at their ignorant behaviour and was wondering whether to make an issue of it. I looked round to see Annie sorting herself out another hit. No support there, then. Now the object of their fun was gone, Sid was back to his usual affable self. Nancy was still agitated at what she saw as an unwelcome intrusion – combined with his failure to recognise them – and kept worrying away at it.

"So who was your old hippy mate, then? Felt like we were fuckin' back at Sid's mom's, ya know? Place full of slobbering old freaks with dope-burns all over their clothes…"

My anger had eased a little. I went over to the record box, rummaging away until I found what I was after. I passed her the LP sleeve, "I'm a bit surprised you didn't recognise *him* actually, Nancy" I said pointing at the sleeve.

She read out loud, "Rainbow Theatre, June 1st, 1974 – Kevin Ayers, John Cale, Eno, Nico … jeez!"

For a second or two she was stunned into silence, before snorting, "You shoulda fuckin' told us, man!"

> *So it begins with a blessing*
> *And it ends with a curse;*
> *Making life easy,*
> *By making it worse;*
> *Just turn to your partner and say*
> *How does it seem? He'll look at you and say*
> *Get out of my dream*
> *Why why why are we sleeping?*

The Uninvited

S id and Nancy were anxious that Annie and I not publicise their presence at our place. This was understandable due to the daily illegalities of our chosen way of life and their infamy. In addition the tabloid press had created a climate where it was physically unsafe for any of the Pistols to be on the street or in public places. Johnny Rotten and Paul Cook had already been subjected to violent attacks by Teds. If word of their presence had got out we'd have had the press and every punk and crazyhead for miles around camped on our squatted doorstep. There was also the possibility that someone would "positively ID" them outside in Eton Avenue. They never considered toning down their act or appearance, and even if they had, it wouldn't have fooled anyone.

Normally we'd have a fairly regular flow of friends; other addicts and hustlers coming round to our place, as well as the overspill from Michael's scene upstairs. For a while things were unusually quiet, until Annie's mate Kathy came over from the big squat on Haverstock Hill looking for a free hit as usual. She could barely contain her excitement when she saw who was there, but they were having one of their introspective days and pretty much ignored her. At least she didn't ask for an autograph. When she left I saw her to the top of the stairs.

"Whatever you do, don't mention them to anyone, okay?"

"Well, alright," she replied, as if she was indulging some very unusual request, "if you say so".

"Look – I know you're cool, but if people know who's

here we'll have half Camden lined up outside."

A couple of days later this got fed back to Annie – apparently I was indicating early signs of coke paranoia but Kathy did keep her word, preferring the quiet satisfaction of keeping a secret to the momentary thrill of disclosure. This could only be a temporary state of affairs, however.

One afternoon we were desperate to escape the bunker-like atmosphere of the flat after an endless circular shouting match between the other two, fading and re-igniting every few minutes. I was pissed off at having to leave my own place to get any peace, but then remembered we hadn't seen our Jamaican mate Jah Tony for a while. Older and wiser than most of our friends, Tony was like a personification of Good Vibes, and I always came away from his place feeling re-charged. He made a living as a musician and always had extraordinarily high quality weed. Heroin was of no interest to him, and although he was aware of our scene he was never judgemental. Generally we'd go round – Annie sometimes taking her guitar – and have a few spliffs, while his tiny Swedish girlfriend flitted about the big open-plan flat, making tea and generally anticipating Tony's needs. Then he'd pick up his guitar and start to play, strumming absent-mindedly at first, sometimes accompanied by a strange little high-pitched hum, until he'd found his direction. From then on I'd be transported down a river of imagination as his music cascaded around us, like a Jamaican John Martyn, briefly freeing us from our daily cares, and reminding us of a better, simpler way. Later, especially after Sid and Nancy had moved on and most of our visitors had lost interest in coming round, we'd wonder why we'd made life so hard for ourselves when all that was really needed were music, natural highs and real friendship.

We rang the bell hoping that he was in, and waited. We were about to leave when the door flew open, Tony standing there with his acoustic in one hand a spliff in the other.

"Hey, wha'appen D!" he laughed, "Mi 'ear you 'ave whole bunch a Sex Pistol livin' round your yard!"

So word was out in the neighbourhood. Naturally Tony was far too cool and sensible to come round and check out the punk rock stars unasked, but he was keen to meet Sid and maybe try some music together. Knowing him to be sensible and trustworthy I agreed – it could have been intriguing, but alas it never happened. Contrary to the received view now that Sid barely knew one end of his bass from another, he used to practice hard most days (at a time when group rehearsals were becoming a rarity). He'd told me before of his Bass Playing Epiphany, speeding out of his head one night, with only a bass and the first Ramones album for company. By dawn he'd cracked it. But he was also eager to explore beyond the Dee Dee Ramone basics of his instrument.

We had most of the ruling reggae singles of '77, all the hot shots: Dr Alimantado, Tapper Zukie, both Roys – I and U, Lee Perry, Prince Jazzbo and Big Youth. The Upsetter's 'Dreadlocks in Moonlight' and the dub side of Bunny Wailer's 'Dreamland' were special favourites of Sid's, though he'd curse them many a time as he tried to play along, head bent over so far in concentration that it was practically in the record player. This could go on for hours as he tried to negotiate the nuances of the dread beat and rhythm. During these times I learnt to be as adept with the arm and stylus as any DJ.

"Just play that last bit again Den – I nearly got the bastard."

Once they'd got established at my place, it seemed futile to maintain the pretence that I had to go out to score. Fortunately this deception garnered respect rather than anger from Sid and Nancy. "Shit, I wouldn't go round tellin' every fuckin' person where I was coppin'," Nancy said, shaking her head in horror at the very idea. But once they started going up to Michael's of their own accord, there was no control over who else might be there. Luckily most of his mates were so retro in their tastes and so disconnected from the music scene that they had only the barest awareness of punk or the Pistols. However, it would only be a matter of time till someone there latched on to Sid's presence, and you could be sure that they wouldn't be cool and considerate like Jah Tony. From then on we knew we had to be ready to deal with the uninvited, and the first such visitor set the tone for much of what was to follow.

Gilly was the chief groveller in Michael's retinue of hangers-on. Small, slight and always eager to please, he bore himself with a cocksure arrogance that came from a privileged upbringing in South Africa – a world of servants and swimming pools. All this came from Daddy being a famous entertainer, "The Man with the Golden Trumpet" one of the main men of Fifties' Easy Listening. Now his son was in London working at becoming "The Man with the Golden Arm". While most of us were living in squats, he had a flat paid for by his family allowance, and our denims and t-shirts were mocked by his feather-cut hair and Kensington Market finery.

I'd first met him a year or so earlier when we'd both been scoring from Rob, one of the dealers down the hill in Camden Town. Gilly would arrive by taxi and sweep in, wearing his new leather blouson, with cord pants tucked into his knee high suede boots. He'd survey the scene disdainfully as he waited to score, reserving special scorn for Rob's untogether girlfriend Caroline, who was meant to answer the door but was invariably gouched out in the corner. In no time Gilly had made himself indispensable, acting like a club doorman, turning away the insolvent and undesirable. For a while Rob's business picked up, but soon the increased turnover and profits led to a rapid increase in his own habit. Gilly sensed that it was time to move on before he got sucked into the increasing chaos at Rob's, and in no time found himself a new position as dealer's lackey with Michael.

So it wasn't that much of a surprise when one day Gilly – now with much shorter hair and straight-legged jeans as a concession to the changing times – opened the door at Michael's. He tried his doorman act with me until The Man called out from within, "Oh it's okay Gilly, that's Denis, send him in".

Michael could still act like a mate when he was in a good mood and not too out of it, but Gilly's arrival marked a downturn in the scene, and soon it was like the court of Macbeth with constant intrigues and petty jealousies. Gilly particularly liked to curry favour by mocking anyone asking for credit. One time I was explaining to Michael when I'd have the cash, before Gilly interrupted with a sneer, "Hey listening to you is like watching someone playing hopscotch in a minefield, Denis".

He reserved a special bitchiness for women, sharing his boss's view that Class A drugs should be left to the boys. Ironically he would eventually lose his post when Michael's girlfriend moved in. Once she'd got a habit she made sure there'd be no-one else between her and the main man, but that was still in the future. One time Annie went up looking for tick while Michael was out. Gilly refused her entry, unless she agreed to let him "show her how to make some money". After that he was barred from coming down to our place. So it was quite surprising when, one Friday night, I answered a knock at the door to find Gilly standing there in the hall with a big grin on his face. I looked him up and down coldly, taking my time, and looking forward to sending him on his way, "What do you want, Gilly? Is your master out or something?"

"No man," he answered quickly, "I was talking to Nancy earlier on and she said to come down and hang out". He looked pleased with himself – clearly this was his trump card, and one I hadn't expected. He carried on as we went down the stairs, "I said I could get them some speed –

sulphate, you know?" It made sense that he'd be one of the first to arrive bearing gifts, practically on his knees. The guy was a born groveller, always latching on to someone else's scene. I did a double-take as he came in from the darkness of the hall. His neatly cut hair was now dyed green with bilious yellow highlights. I ignored him as he chattered on. "I'm really looking forward to talking to Sid about music. Maybe we could do something together, you know…". My heart sank. A visitor I couldn't stand bringing my least favourite drug. If they did a load of speed we'd probably be stuck with the little git all night, talking shit in his grating accent.

Nancy was at the table in the corner, doing her eye make-up in between talking to Annie, her face sandwiched between the table lamp and her mirror as she made sure of every detail. Sid was sitting on our bed, watching TV and half-heartedly plucking at his bass. He looked up briefly to acknowledge Gilly with a grunt, then carried on. Annie flashed a glare at me, but before she could say anything Nancy called out, without looking up, "So didja get it then, mate?" in her best Cockney-light voice.

"Sure did, it's good stuff too," he replied.

Nancy looked up, and paused for a second before saying, "Jeez, what happened to your hair? Was someone sick on you?"

Gilly tried to laugh it off and sat down. He reached into his shirt pocket and casually flipped a small packet on to the table, then made a great show of refusing any payment for it. Turning to me, he smiled and said, "I'm sorry, there isn't enough for you guys though".

"Don't worry, I don't want any of your speed anyway Gilly," I replied.

From then on the room split into two separate camps. Annie and I withdrew into the cave-like structure around our bed, while Gilly and the others sat over the other side of the room and shot up their speed. It didn't appear to have much effect on Sid. After an initial burst of chat he seemed to be quieter than usual if anything. As I'd feared, Gilly went into a monologue, showing off and name-dropping all the music biz big names he'd met and hung out with. I noticed Nancy looking over at us and rolling her eyes. I smiled back thinking, well, you invited him…

After a while she got out her prized photo and cuttings album, not so much to impress Gilly as to gain a respite from his grating chatter. For a while things went quieter, save for Nancy's husky drawl, "This one's by Bob Gruen, the Dolls' photographer – ya heard of him, right? Yeah, that's me, and the other guys are Steven Tyler and Joe Perry from Aerosmith, and this one's Allen Lanier from Blue Oyster Cult. You know who Freddie Sessler is?"

Coming back from the toilet, Gilly spotted Annie's guitar propped against the wall and snatched it up without asking. I'd been waiting for him to step out of line, and was about to pounce, but Annie beat me to it, "You break it, you pay for it. I'm watching you".

He dropped down beside Sid, who drew back as Gilly had a brief thrash at the guitar, "You want to have a jam, Sid? Maybe we could write a song together?".

For the first time that night I sensed that Sid was becoming irritated by our visitor. I hoped that Gilly would prattle on until he'd be swiftly silenced by a blow from Sid's studded belt. However, he was in a strangely subdued mood, leaving most of the talking to Nancy, and simply shook his head. Undeterred, Gilly chattered on, "That's okay Sid. Listen, there's a song I'm working on, I'll play it and see what you think…"

I'd had no idea he had any musical pretensions before. Maybe Gilly had hidden talents inherited from his father. He started to play what was meant to be a punky riff, and soon he was approaching a chorus;

"I ain't got no money/ I can't get no job/ Cos I'm so fucked up…"

The dirge continued on its inexorable journey. By the time of the third verse –

"She said she loved me/ I know it isn't true/ Cos she's too fucked up…"

I realised the song was going to work through each personal pronoun, with a subtle variation to the last line of each verse. By this time Nancy had returned to fixing her make-up, and Sid had come over to our space on the pretext of wanting a fag.

Finally Gilly made it over the finishing line, "… And they're always fucked up"

He looked around for applause that never came. Annie moved across the room with a speed I'd rarely seen before, grabbed back her guitar and joined Nancy by the spotlight to examine it for any scratches or other damage.

Naturally Gilly was oblivious to any changes in the mood of the evening. By now it was around midnight. "Hey it's still early – you guys want to go out to a club or something? I know a few places – or maybe we could go to The Roxy or The Vortex? What do you say, Sid?"

Sid squinted at Gilly, seemingly more alert now, and started to smile, "That fucking toilet? You're having a laugh aren't you?"

We couldn't help laughing out loud. Gilly tried to hide his discomfort, before making his excuses and getting up to leave, "Is that the time? I'd better see what's happening up at Michael's. It's been great meeting you Sid, do it again sometime…"

I saw him up the stairs to the front door. To my amazement he suddenly started acting like we were mates. Didn't he have any awareness or self-respect?

"Good one Denis. I'll get enough speed for everyone next time. I'll bring some grass from home too – DP, Durban Poison, you know?"

It was too much of an open goal. I knew there'd be comebacks, but I couldn't resist it.

"There won't be a next time Gilly. I don't like you and I don't like speed, okay?"

He looked surprised and lost for a moment, the spoilt rich kid used to getting his own way. I thought he was going to say something, but he slipped out into the dark hall and left silently. I went back down to find the others preparing a hit. I waited until Nancy seemed fairly mellow before saying, "I'd rather you didn't ask that guy down here again…"

Nancy shrugged her shoulders without looking up, and I sensed her bristle slightly when she replied, "I asked him down? I don't remember – but if you say so, yeah, yeah". At last the place was quiet. I was about to lie back with Annie, when Nancy spoke again, "But yeah, he was kinda an asshole…" Gilly committed suicide by drug overdose in Chelsea a few years later, citing boredom as the main reason.

After a while the novelty of our unusual domestic set-up wore off for our local friends and we were generally undisturbed. But as always fate had the odd wild card to play and this duly came in the form of an incongruous clash of past and present scenes. Cambridge seemed like it existed in a distant age; if I thought of those times at all, it felt more like remembering someone else's life than my own. Most people had moved on or were wise enough to steer clear of our twilight zone but occasionally the two worlds would overlap.

There was my old drug-buddy Richard, a stylish character who always had the best hash, the latest sounds, and held court to the cooler people on the Cambridge alternative scene. I was first introduced to coke at his afternoon salon. Sure, he was basically another rich kid with an inflated sense of entitlement, but there was a devil-may-care *joie de vivre* attitude to him that I always liked. Sitting around in stoned silence was anathema to Richard, and there'd always be lively debates on the topics of the day, such as the respective merits of Jefferson Airplane and the Grateful Dead. Richard would hold forth, like the barrister he was training to be, "I put it to you man, that the Dead shit on the Airplane from a great height every fucking time. I have checked them both out under the influence of the highest possible stimulant – by which I mean LSD – and it's no contest, I assure you".

After uni he was off on the Afghan Trail and stayed away for over a year. I next met him round my usual dealer's place not long after he got back, still dressed in his Afghan robe, much quieter than before, apart from the occasional assenting "acha". Previously he'd always rejected opiates and their users, but it didn't take long to establish the source of his private smile and spaced-out demeanour. We resumed our drug-buddy friendship and pursued our new interest in opiates, though he at least had the wisdom not to shoot up. We were still mainly weekend dabblers then, holding down straight jobs all week. At Cambridge he'd always had a sharp wit about the absurd and artificial aspects of the place, "It's just a big play-pen, man, where you can do pretty much as you want for three years and everyone's super-nice to you – then you get out into the real world. Big shock, man…"

Working at the merchant bank soon changed his outlook, though, as he informed me one night, "Look man, we aren't eighteen any more. There comes a point where you have to decide whether you're going to be one of the Haves or one of the Have-Nots. I know which I want."

So while Annie and I were living in our squat, Richard and his girlfriend Sarah were buying a sumptuous flat in a Hampstead mansion block. One Saturday we'd arrived to find the place awash with kittens and Richard exasperated by the little black bundles of life hurtling round the room, up and down the new velvet curtains and exploring every forbidden place. It was inevitable that when we left we'd be taking one of them home with us. The kitten fitted neatly into Annie's pocket for the journey home. I was informed that she was to be known as "Misha", Italian for "pussycat". Once we got back she made a cursory exploration of the flat, and after a saucer of milk, decided it was to her liking. Probably taken from her mother a bit too soon, she bonded intensely with Annie, and got to be great mates with Sid and Nancy, who appreciated her punky independent attitude.

One night we were talking in bed and close to drifting off, when Annie told me how she'd met Sarah for coffee and invited her over to see how much Misha had grown. I was about to reply when she added, "Oh, by the way it kind of slipped out that Sid and Nancy are here now" – I grunted in disapproval – "Don't worry, it'll be okay".

I wasn't so sure. Richard could be great company and liked nothing more than telling a good story, but generally expected to be the centre of attention. His musical tastes were still largely dictated by *Rolling Stone* magazine and the *Old Grey Whistle Test*. There was also an element of tourism which worried me too. Then again, maybe the shared goal of Getting Stoned would over-ride any problems. We were sitting round stoned a few nights later when they turned up. I could tell straight away that Richard's plummy accent and casual confidence irritated Sid, who looked scornfully at the oh-so-small and tasteful ear-piercing, and carefully blow-dried mid-length hair. This look might have been pretty radical at the bank where he worked, but was about as punk as the Queen's Christmas Message. Settling down next to Nancy on the settee, he pulled out a chunk of hash and threw it in my direction with the command, "Put one together, man" – faux pas number one of the evening.

Richard had always been an avid reader of the music press and trade papers, and liked to name-drop various business insiders he happened to know. He went into barrister mode and started quizzing Sid for the inside story of the Pistols and their rapid succession of record labels, culminating in, "So what about America, then?"

Sid was bored but reasonably polite as he answered, limiting himself to occasional brief replies or shrugs. I could tell Nancy was feeling left out as she shifted restlessly, disdainfully refusing the joint I'd rolled. Although she felt the impromptu interview was intrusive, she was disappointed by Sid's cursory replies. At first she corrected the odd detail or omission, but then took over, giving Richard a rambling account of the group's past, present and future, in which she was a major player, "I was telling Malcolm, like yeah, the group was great to begin with, but Glen wanted it to be like the fuckin' Beatles, you know? And with Johnny Rotten it was just one front-man – now my Sidney's there and the kids love him right off, it's like Richard Hell and Johnny Thunders in the Heartbreakers…"

After a while Richard caught my eye with a conspiratorial look that I knew well, and after waiting for a suitably dramatic moment, enquired, "Do you happen to have a spare mirror by any chance?"

I noticed Sid and Nancy exchanging glances of distaste, noses wrinkling.

Annie fetched the big mirror Nancy used for her make-up. Richard placed it across his lap, and with a dramatic flourish produced a fold of white paper from his Levi's shirt pocket,

"Anyone want to do some coke, then?"

I could see Annie's face light up. Suddenly she was leaning forward a little from the edge of her seat as Richard tipped out some of the powder. Heroin might be Number One Drug now by necessity, but she'd always had a liking for cocaine when it was around. I remembered the last time we'd had some at her folks' in Brighton, when her father had been moved to comment, "You seem to have a smile like an alligator today, my dear."

The other two maintained their indifference. Unperturbed, Richard produced a blade and started chopping up the gear. To him it was like being the cool dealer hanging out with the Stones in the Sixties, his drugs and connections putting him on an equal level with any rock star, passing or permanent. At first there was something pleasing about the ritual and the rapid rhythmic chopping sound of the blade on the mirror. But every time I thought he was about to serve up the lines, he'd scrape the coke back into a little central pile and start the whole process again. It was his gear so I couldn't say anything. Nancy stamped off to the toilet dramatically, muttering to herself. Eventually Richard rolled up a banknote and scarfed up the largest of the six lines, before passing the mirror to Sarah, indicating a particularly dainty line for her. When it reached us, I looked down to see the smallest, thinnest filigree lines ever – but Annie and I snorted ours without complaint like the well brought-up children we were.

When I passed the mirror on to Nancy I could see she'd already sized up the situation. I started to feel uneasy. Generally cocaine was a fun social drug – all about staying up late, ranting and talking nonsense with mates, or fuelling marathon backgammon sessions. But there was a downside where things could go off track, and once started it was hard to recover. Antagonism and paranoia would take over, with small suspicions and imagined slights leading to serious discord.

"Sheesh, there's not much here," she said, her eyes only a few inches from the mirror, as if that was the only way she could actually discern the micro-line. Sid leant across, feigning an exaggerated display of peering intently at the mirror.

"Hey, can you put out some more? I'm not even going to feel that," Nancy asked Richard, now rolling a joint.

"Well actually I was saving some for later, you know".

Sid and Nancy looked at each other, exasperated. Suddenly Richard snatched the mirror back, pulled out the little packet and tipped out a bit more coke.

"There you go man," he said through clenched teeth,

like a tetchy teacher.

They homed in together over the mirror.

"Hey well if that's all there fucking is, I'll have to bang it up," announced Nancy, getting up to look for her outfit. Richard hated anything to do with needles, and shifted uncomfortably to let Nancy past. But his troubles had only just begun.

Sid looked up, fixing him with a lopsided glare, and said, "Look mate, if you're going to give us some fucking coke, at least give us enough to fucking feel it."

Richard harrumphed, "Well, that looks like plenty to me".

Sid carried on grumbling, this time about some of the Pistols' fashion-crowd hangers-on who always made a big deal about having loads of coke, but were too dumb to realise their gear was crap. By now Nancy was back with their syringes and the rest of the injecting kit. For a few moments they were quiet, working as a team as they scraped the coke from the mirror to a spoon, then preparing and measuring their hits. Once the process was complete, they disengaged into separate mode, scrutinising each other's outfits to make sure neither had more. Normally shooting up coke produces an instant brain-rattling rush. I noticed Richard's uncomfortable look and waited to see what would happen.

"Fuck, didn't feel a thing," cursed Sid.

"Well maybe I mighta felt a tiny little buzz, if I really try," drawled Nancy, before gaining momentum, "Ya still got some of that shit left. I really wanna feel a fucking buzz. And give Denis and Annie some more too".

I noticed Richard flush for a moment and could see he was finding it hard to keep his temper. Looking flustered, he snapped, "Coke's quite expensive, you know. I wanted to take some home.

Sid rummaged in his leather jacket and pulled out some crumpled notes. "Well, fucking sell us some then. I dunno

why you come round with coke and then get all fucking
mean with it. You're wasting our time and your coke – and
you're making a cunt of yourself too."

Richard looked stunned. They didn't act like that at
Cambridge or the merchant bank. His face reddened
again. Then he gulped, before replying indignantly, "Well,
there is such a thing as a bit of gratitude when someone
turns you on".

Now Nancy moved in for the kill, "Yeah sure, but you
haven't turned us on. A fucking baby wouldn't have felt
what you gave us."

All the while we'd been silent onlookers with Sarah.
Suddenly she'd had enough and stood up quickly, grabbing
her things as she did so.

"Come on, it's getting late, we've got work tomorrow."

Richard objected briefly, then admitted defeat. To my
surprise, he tossed the little packet on to the mirror, and
tried to sound cool and detached as he forced a wan smile,
"Well, I guess you guys might as well finish that off".

Sid and the others pounced on the packet like vultures,
while I went upstairs with Richard and Sarah to see them
out. When we were in the hall, Richard turned to me and
put on his most sonorous "I'm Being Serious Now" voice,
"Well Denis, I came here tonight with an open mind. I'd
heard some bad things about your new friend. And I have
to say my worst fears were confirmed."

A Night At The Marquee

When Sid and Nancy moved into our place I imagined that our social life would take a dramatic upturn. We'd be clubbing, gigging, ligging, drugging and generally hanging out punk rock style. It soon became clear that on Sid's meagre allowance from the Pistols, we'd be lucky to manage a night at the pub. They'd experienced threats and harassment when out, and besides, there are few things more conducive to an indoor lifestyle than a heroin habit.

Yet from time to time we did venture out into the uncomprehending world. One crisp autumn afternoon – to our total surprise – they announced that they wanted to join us on the weekly trip to the launderette down the road. Despite all the arguments and casual violence, there was a *Babes in the Wood* side to Sid and Nancy where they'd go all sentimental, and play out the roles of mainstream Mummies and Daddies, briefly immersing themselves in the mundane routines of living as a couple. Generally Nancy seemed to be the dominant one in the relationship, telling us with relish that Sid had been "practically a virgin" when they met, and that she'd taught him all he knew about sex – not that he seemed to mind. Occasionally he'd object, saying that he'd had plenty of previous girlfriends and sexual encounters, but they'd all been "dogs" compared to Nancy, the first partner to really engage him emotionally and sexually. But sometimes she could sink into a childlike neediness – maybe, we'd call it "being high maintenance" now – and out of nowhere there'd be a sudden asthma attack, followed by a series of dramas around finding her inhalers before calm would return.

When we got to the launderette in England's Lane it was busy, with machines clanking and humming, while the regulars caught up on local gossip. Nancy suddenly developed a great interest in the small details of the laundry, using her Dickensian Cockney Waif voice and discussing the merits of conditioners and water-softeners with one of the customers. No-one took any notice of us, and once we'd loaded our washing – comprising Pistols' and Heartbreakers' t-shirts for the most part – into a couple of machines I went and bought some Cokes at the shop next door. As it was stuffy and noisy in the launderette we decided to take our drinks to the bus shelter round the corner while the washing went round. Being mid-afternoon the street was soon swarming with kids coming out of the local schools. In no time they spotted Sid, and after some nervous whispering, they started to come over.

The boldest girl stepped forward, after carefully mussing up her hair, "My mate reckons you're Sid Vicious, but I ain't sure…"

Sid laughed, "Neither am I most of the time…"

His identity established, Sid fielded a deluge of breathless questions.

"When you playing live again?"

"What's the next record mate?"

Soon he was signing every scrap of paper, exercise book or school bag pushed his way. When there was nothing left to sign he ended up taking the badges off his jacket for them. Sid had often talked about how the group's fans – especially the young ones – were what mattered most to him, more than the music, money or drugs. He was adamant that he'd never succumb to the Star Trip and distance himself from the kids. There was an idealistic side to Sid which he usually kept well hidden, or got lost in the endless piss-taking banter of his day-to-day conversation. It was great to see that he really meant it and it was moving to see how much the kids responded to his openness.

Initially Nancy was delighted by the happy throng milling around us in the shelter, as it lent support to her claim – advanced more and more often now – that Sid was more popular with the kids than Johnny Rotten, and this was because their uncontaminated minds could tell that Sid was "for real", while the singer had now sold out in his desire for stardom. Soon though it became clear that there was no fame-by-association. Annie and I barely merited a glance, despite our leather jackets and Pistols shirts. Nancy pushed her way into the crowd, thinking they'd soon be wanting her autograph too. After all she was a star now as well, right? But the kids weren't interested, her embarrassment only saved by a bus coming round the corner. Suddenly the kids were gone, but we weren't alone for long.

Two local old girls arrived, wheezing and puffing on their fags, clad in hats and coats despite the warm weather, and pushing fearsome wheeled shopping trolleys before them. These were used as battering rams to shunt us down into the far end of the bus shelter. After a while it was impossible to ignore the glares directed at us, followed by a stage-whispered conversation, "It's 'im innit, that Sex Pistol. Vicious or sumfing…"

"Ooh yeah, you're right. Don't 'e look 'orrible…"

A while later we were snug again down in the basement. Sid was reading the *NME* between nods, checking out the live section. Suddenly he spotted that X-Ray Spex were playing The Marquee that night, and he wanted to go. A couple of phone calls later and transport and guest-list had been arranged. This was all a little surprising, as Sid usually had nothing but scorn for most UK punk groups. Clearly X-Ray Spex were among the exceptions. For our part, we'd bought a couple of their singles, and Annie loved Poly Styrene's hi-concept appearance and don't-give-a-toss vibe – I wasn't so sure. There were so many groups around at the time with a good song or two, striking looks and a bit of attitude, but nothing much beyond that. Even at that early stage there was a clear hierarchy emerging on the punk scene – were X-Ray Spex going to rise to the elite or drift along in Division Two with the likes of Generation X or Eddie and the Hot Rods.

Although The Ramones always came first for him, Sid was passionately loyal to old mates where groups were concerned. So he loved The Slits, on account of the Flowers of Romance connection via Viv Albertine. There was a kind of grudging respect for The Clash. I was relieved that my own favourites – The Only Ones – merited a nod of approval. As for The Hot Rods, there'd been friction between them and the Pistols when they'd been on the same live bill – and were bandwagon-jumping pop lightweights in Sid's opinion, to be cast into oblivion along with such opportunists as The Police or The Vibrators. Generation X were particularly scorned – there seemed to be a very personal animosity towards Billy Idol – as copyists and for looking, in his words, like "mail order punks". His loathing of The Damned had a similar edge to it. Elvis Costello wasn't punk in any way, I was told firmly. The Jam were mere Sixties revivalists, while The Stranglers were so old as to be barely worthy of consideration as "punk" – or as Nancy put it once, their fans were "the kinda people who go to football matches", much to my chagrin. There was no denying that we had both The Stranglers' albums and I tried to mount a defence. My turning point in getting into punk – rather than just liking some of the singles because they reminded me of The Who or Small Faces – had come at the Roundhouse in summer '76. We'd gone to see long term favourite Patti Smith. Since the arrival of *Horses* at the beginning of that year we'd sought out books of hers like *Seventh Heaven*, and then obscure import singles and US magazines. She'd been amazing, and as we'd spent the whole set pressed against the front of the stage. We'd been blown away by the sheer physicality and dervish energy of the music as much as the power and intensity of the lyrics. However I'd been just as impressed by how The Stranglers handled a disinterested and increasingly hostile crowd who were only interested in seeing the Big Name they'd paid money for. It was one of the most dramatic and intense gigs I've ever seen – or "dialectical", as Jean-Jacques Burnel had put it at the time – but Sid and Nancy were unmoved. The Stranglers had been marked down as provincial dinosaurs, and there could be no way back, Nancy ending all discussion with a dismissive, "They're just too old, you know?" with a slight shudder at the thought.

For once Nancy managed to sort out her clothes, hair, make-up and sprays in time, and all that was left to do was to have a serious hit to set us up for the rest of the evening. The Post Office Tower once again signed the way like a beacon as we drifted down from Camden towards the West End. I recalled how it had lit the way home the night we'd all met, and how distant the summer seemed now.

Going to The Marquee… I drifted back to my first visit in March '68, seeing Ten Years After with a bunch of mates from school, carrying our cool clothes round with us all day in anticipation. I'd smoked my first joint during a frantic pre-gig session round at Steve's house before his folks got in from work. From then on it became a regular hang-out on my weekend live music scene. All those British Blues Boom groups – John Mayall, Jethro Tull, Chicken Shack, Fleetwood Mac – seemed like something from another life time now, less than a decade later.

I pulled out of my reverie as the cab jolted to a halt in Wardour Street. For all the changes in music and fashion since then, the queue for The Marquee huddled on the pavement was the same, stretching down the road and trying to keep out the cold. We disgorged ourselves from the back of the car and stepped out unsteadily. We were spotted straight-away. It seemed like a pretty even split between friendly cries of "Hey Sid – over 'ere mate" or "Hey, can you get us in?" and some harsher shouts of "Wanker – Bitch – Slag" and, "Oi, got yer drugs 'ave you?" (yes, we had, since you asked).

Although there were no flashbulbs popping or eager reporters thrusting mics in our faces, one of my mundane guest-list fantasies came true as we walked straight to the head of the line, and with Sid being one of the most recognisable faces in London, we were ushered into the narrow entrance corridor without any problem. It had been a while since I'd been to The Marquee, but the décor was unchanged – those same red and white stripes on the wall – and it didn't look like they'd had the cleaners in since last time either. The club was struggling to adapt to the punk scene and a different set of groups, fans and customs. Tonight though the audience was probably divided pretty equally between healthy looking blonde Scandinavian students, tourists, and the local punks.

We'd missed the support group, and soon X-Ray Spex came on, Poly Styrene bursting on to the stage in an explosion of synthetic material, acidic colours and trademark teeth-braces. But there was a vulnerable feeling to her alongside the brashness. Alas it wasn't the original line-up with Lora Logic on sax, but they did have some seriously good songs. Apart from 'Oh Bondage', there was 'Identity', 'The Day the World Turned Day-Glo', and 'Germ Free Adolescents;, which all sounded great despite problems with the crap PA. The new sax player was probably a bit too keen to show his worth and tended to blast all over everything, not helped by a sound-mix that reduced everything else to a cement-mixer chug. All a great shame, as otherwise they had the tightness that only comes from putting in the hard yards on the road. I looked round at Annie and saw she was beaming with pleasure, eyes rapt on Poly Styrene. The rows of little plastic seats that used to be in front of the stage were long gone, the space now occupied by a heaving mass of Sid's dreaded "mail order punks", pogoing and gobbing because that was what you were meant to do at a punk gig, right?

I was just thinking how different it was from the days when almost everyone sat on the floor at gigs, and tried to remember when it had become so totally uncool as it was now, when Sid leant over and yelled into my ear, "Oi, do you wanna get a beer?"

We pushed our way through the crowd at the back of the club. Eventually we got there only to be ignored by the bar staff who weren't going to give any special service to someone just because he was a Sex Pistol. Finally we grabbed our bottles of Pils and headed towards a grimy fag-scarred sofa at the back of the room. I'd noticed a few double-takes while we were waiting at the bar, and now word was definitely out about Sid's presence. Soon people were edging closer all around us.

It was the first time we'd sat down since arriving, and I could feel the lurking smack buzz hit me full force. I looked round at the others, struggling to fight the nod and focus my vision as I did so. Annie was first to go as always, and was soon resting her head on my shoulder in a deep gouch. Sid was sprawled back, mouth ajar, but somehow holding his beer bottle upright with deeply stoned skill. All I could make out of Nancy was the back of her head, hair in disarray, slumped down low between her knees, her breathing hoarse and erratic.

I must have nodded out myself for a few minutes, only coming round when my cigarette burnt down to my fingers. It looked like the scene in an old film where someone wakes up after being knocked out. There was a weird fish-eye lens quality to my field of vision, a bit blurred, and with everything seeming to crowd in towards me from the edges. We were framed by a light I hadn't noticed before above the sofa, highlighting us in the general gloom of the club. There seemed something almost pre-Raphaelite about the composition of this scene, a strange innocence amid the squalor. I started to drift off again but forced myself back. I looked up and realised that the onlookers had edged closer. Now people were whispering and pointing in our direction, although no-one addressed us directly.

"What do you reckon?"

"Well, it does look like him"

"Nah, it's just some look-alike"

"Yeah, but that looks like her too…."

"Wow, they look really out of it"

"And he's really fucked…"

It started to feel like being an animal at the zoo. I'd always been scornful of the so-called "pressures of stardom" but being owned and discussed by all-comers wasn't my idea of fun. As I tried to stir Annie I was aware of flashbulbs popping close by. I've often wondered who took those pictures and what became of them, as they've never surfaced to my knowledge. Probably long lost, or buried deep in some forgotten Scandinavian scrapbook.

Now Sid came round, his mood changing as soon as he saw the cameras. "Come on Nance, we're going", he said, roughly shaking her awake, before pushing past a couple of French punks wanting autographs. He was in a foul mood all the way home. Once again, being a star had failed to deliver.

Autumn Days

It was great having Annie back, but it had seemed strange at first. For a couple of weeks there'd been just the three of us at the flat, but now there were two couples and four habits contained in the one room. Sometimes life would assume a mutated playroom vibe, dressing-up box courtesy of Sex – apart from our own clothes, a kind of communal heap of garments had evolved, operating as a punk pick and mix selection. Sometimes I'd get lucky and stride down the road wearing one of Sid's spare leather jackets, but I'd often get the short straw of a very itchy pink mohair sweater with one black sleeve. Sometimes it felt like a smacked-out Enid Blyton story: the *Fucked-Up Four And Their Daily Survival Adventures*.

Soon though it all seemed normal enough, and given that the house had been totally infiltrated over the years by all manner of squatters, dopers and other outlaws, no-one was likely to take that much interest as long as we didn't do anything to attract attention. A kind of routine developed where I'd usually be the first up and off down the hill to collect our methadone from Hall's at Chalk Farm. I'd pick up essentials like milk, coffee and fags on the way back. Sometimes I'd get a *Guardian* or magazine too. When I got back I'd feel like Father Christmas as the three faces looked up at me expectantly.

"Did you get my Twix?"

"No *Melody Maker* then?"

Occasionally there'd be a drama – like the time the carrier bag broke, leaving an unappetising milk and methadone mix in the gutter – but for a lot of the time

life settled into a routine. Sid was frequently away on
group business – although he was often the only one to
turn up for practices – from which Nancy was pointedly
excluded. There'd been a kind of honeymoon period to
begin with, when they seemed to be the embodiment of
Young Love. Although they'd both close ranks ferociously
against anyone who gave them trouble, arguments and
fights were becoming pretty regular, with Nancy usually the
instigator, railing against what she saw as Sid's passivity and
indecision. There was always a potential for claustrophobic
tensions with four of us living at such close quarters. When
the arguments started we'd sometimes take cover in the
bunker-like space of the bed-platform, trying to ignore
the hissed and whispered conversations from the other
side of the room. Sid's absences would nearly always be
the cause of some drama, but once he was away Nancy
would often seem a lot more relaxed, catching up with some
other expatriate punk girlfriends, or enjoying more endless
discussions about books, films and music – and of course
the perennial topic, "Why is life so crap?"

Solo time – individual or as a twosome – was impossible.
Matters came to a head one nightmarish Sunday afternoon.
Sid was being picked up next morning and would be away
for a gig. We'd been aware of trouble brewing – especially a
simmering sexual tension – for a couple of days, in the form
of constant little digs and asides from Nancy. She was feeling
unappreciated and frustrated, the situation not helped by
Sid's main interest being in rounding up enough drugs to
take away with him. We'd made a couple of tactical exits –
making it clear we'd be out for a while (which was a relief in
itself) – in the hope that we'd find everything to have been
"consummately" resolved, as it were, on our return.

When we got back – coughing loudly from the top of the
stairs before descending – the atmosphere was poisonous.
Nancy was stamping around in her underwear, berating
and taunting Sid, who sat on the bed looking miserable, but

clearly in an equally foul mood.

I could see a grim night ahead, and tried to catch Annie's eye to indicate it'd be best to go out again. However she'd nested straight away, grabbing her stash tin, lighting a fag, turning on the television and getting settled on our bed. We tried to insulate ourselves in our little cave but it was impossible to ignore Nancy as she got louder and more personal.

Sid resumed his efforts, but by now nothing he could do was right.

"I could fuckin' do that better myself," she snarled at any foreplay suggestions. Finally Sid announced he was ready for action, only for her to sneer, "What am I supposed to do with that little willy!"

"Fuck you, we're gonna do fucking everything if you just shut up for a minute!"

It was no surprise though that Sid's efforts came to nought.

"You lost it already! You hardly got in for fuck's sake!" Nancy shouted, grabbing the sheet and wrapping it round her as she stormed off to the bathroom.

Annie would sometimes stay over with her friends in Tufnell Park. Chief among these was her old college friend, Ella. This was very much a solo trip. Ella and I had never got on, even in the laidback country cottage days of "Hey we're all friends, man". It was a succession of little things to begin with. She had a squeaky, high-pitched, whiny voice which really grated. I couldn't stand her taste in music either, with many a psych-out session derailed by her suddenly interposing *Tea for the Tillerman*, *Tapestry* or *Ladies of the Canyon*. Soon snide little comments – always behind my back – started to filter back to me, followed by pointed non-invitations to meals and gigs with the rest of the crowd.

Her dislike of me intensified when I was seen as having taken her best friend from her, and this was soon elaborated into a theory that I'd got Annie into hard drugs as a first step to having my way with her and having her under my thumb from then on. It would always take Annie and me a day or two to get back on track together after one of her visits and to undo the effect of all Ella's manipulative guilt-tripping.

Nancy kept her head down reading the music papers as Annie and I went through the standard pre-Tufnell Park visit routine and argument. Like Sid, she wanted supplies to take with her. This could lead to all kinds of trouble with Ella.

"Look, try and keep it together when you're there. Don't get too stoned and gouch all over the place, don't spend ages in the bathroom having a hit – I don't need her rubbishing me all over town again."

Once Annie had left, we turned off the television and listened to music. Given the preponderance of Ramones, Dolls, Richard Hell, Blondie and, of course, the Heartbreakers in their collection there was a strong New York flavour to Nancy's choices. I'd been talking for a while about John Cale's solo albums, and came back at her with tracks from *Paris 1919*, *Fear* and *Slow Dazzle*. We had our drugs for the night, enough but not too much, and soon I was telling her all about my New York trip in '73, especially how I'd taken the word of a music business old hand I'd met and thus missed out on seeing the Dolls at the Mercer Arts Center. "They'll never amount to anything," he'd assured me as we went to see Maria Muldaur instead.

We'd been discussing a recent article in *NME*, where Tony James from Generation X and Mick Jones had been talking about the difference between punk bands and the established scene, opining that they couldn't imagine going to see anyone who was fat or old, when Nancy suddenly leant forward and said "Well yeah – don't get me wrong, but you should really do something about your hair, ya know? Gimme some scissors and I'll fix it for ya."

I was a bit surprised, and then amused by this. My old hirsute look was long gone, replaced by a fairly typical nondescript mid-length style that had been acceptable for work but that subtly hinted at some individuality under the surface – or so I hoped. In terms of pure millimetre-count, Sid's hair was actually longer than mine – quite at odds with the tabloid press "Guide to Punk Rockers" orthodoxy that punk hair was always spiky and short. If in doubt, check how rarely you can see Sid's ears in any photos you come across. There was no denying though that his black crown had a panache and identity to which I could only aspire. Naturally Nancy claimed credit for the look that had transformed Sid from loser squatter to punk rock star. It'd be a cool surprise for Annie when she came back and, anyway, it sounded better than another night gouching in front of the television.

"Sure, you got anything in mind?" I replied.

"That fuckin' fringe has gotta go, ya know? You got quite a strong face, you don't need hair all over it. Maybe a kinda James Dean Fifties look? Bit like Joe Strummer, whaddya reckon?"

It sounded fine to me, so while she rummaged in her bags for some scissors I pulled a chair into the middle of the room so that it was under the light. Soon she was snipping away intently. I liked the idea that I was being shorn by the very same scissors that cut Sid's hair. She moved surely and confidently, her bleached frizz contrasting with her standard black day-to-day outfit. Once she'd got into the rhythm of her cutting we started talking again. I liked the way her fingers moved strongly and expertly across my head, and how her little black and silver pistol neck-chain bobbed away cheekily as she moved. Eventually she was standing in front of me. Wearing the loose black shirt familiar from many a photo, she swayed back and forth as she cut and talked, usually managing somehow to smoke a fag hands-free at the same time. As she leant forward it was impossible to ignore her breasts or the beguiling cleavage, often only inches from my face. I wasn't going to make a move on her, but at the same time I had a feeling that something was going to happen.

There was no way their narco-sexual problems could have been kept secret at such close quarters, Nancy had also picked up on certain tensions between Annie and I. It wasn't unusual for Annie to be too stoned to bother with getting undressed at bedtime, slumping under the duvet, jeans and all, usually gouching with a fag hanging from her mouth, poised to burn holes in anything within range. In addition, she'd started scoring heavy Mandrax downers from one of the squats on the hill, just to ensure oblivion.

We kept the New York musical theme going with the Dolls' albums, which she held in the kind of reverence that Sid reserved for The Ramones. At times it was hard to keep up with the rapid flow of gigs, clubs, scenes, and yet more groups, many so transient I'd never heard of them. One moment she'd be telling me her scabrous tales of being taken under Debbie Harry's wing when she first got to the city, taking in hanging out with Richard Hell and Tom Verlaine in the early days, then she'd be off on another tangent about The Mumps, "That was my friend Lance's group. Lance Loud, you know? The guy I told you about who brought me round when I nearly died on that red Puerto Rican shit?" – she could be quite strict, making sure I was paying attention – "You really remind me of him – me and Lance would just stay up forever, talking about books and movies."

As so often, we'd end up with the Heartbreakers' album *L.A.M.F.* (NYC abbreviation for "Like a Motherfucker"). We loved it, but there was no denying the weak and tinny production that marred the record. Unable to get their first choice producer, the group had bizarrely ended up using Thunderclap Newman's guitarist, Speedy Keene (or "Weedy Keene" as Nancy called him). Gradually I was drawn ever deeper into the album, as songs and characters were explained and expanded on. These stories would often focus on the group's guitarist, the legendary Johnny Thunders, who sadly and mysteriously died in 1991. She'd generally refer to him just as "Thunders", which seemed to convey extra respect. One time she'd spent a whole morning showing Sid, Annie and I all the Thunders-approved ways of tying a bandanna, garter – or whatever else came to hand – around your leg, and then did it look better tied mid-thigh or round a boot-top? The man was one of those natural embodiments of Cool, whose look and style pretty much started where Keith Richards had left off.

As always, though, with Nancy there were other nuances to her stories. She shared my liking for Hubert Selby's *Last Exit to Brooklyn* and I'd often think back to that book with a shudder as she'd tell me about her Puerto Rican pimp raping her with a broomstick for not bringing back enough money. Equally, for all that she sometimes seemed in awe of Thunders as a paragon of cool style, drugs and music, she'd add that at heart he was still the basic New York Italian home boy – Johnny Genzale – expecting to come home to his dinner on the table while his woman attended to the *bambini*.

I'd always loved the Dolls' song, 'Subway Train' – it was one of the sounds that instantly took me back to my time in New York – but the Heartbreakers' version took the song to another level. Thunders' singing contained a perfect mix of desperation, resignation and defiance which emphasised the power of the lyrics. Nancy carefully explained it all, till I knew the identity of the recipient of the "epic letter that never got sent," "Miss Rosie", and why Thunders considered his life to be "cursed, poisoned and condemned." Another track I loved was 'It's Not Enough' – which sounds like an out-take from the Stones' *Out of Our Heads* album, endless twelve-string reverb and echo to go with his yearning voice – where Thunders had transformed the aches and despair of being strung out into an intense love song. Even so, it didn't stop Sid from taking the piss whenever we played the album, saying, "I've got to tell him – he sounds just like that old poof Jagger there!"

By then the first hints of dawn were intruding. We sat on the edge of the bed, having a last hit and trying to keep up an increasingly fractured conversation. There'd been no element of seduction in our talk, but for an hour or so I'd known that the night wasn't going to end with us chastely retiring to our separate sides of the room. I was just finishing my fag, when she said, "Is it okay if I stay over here tonight? It's been really good talking and I don't wanna be on my own now. You know how some things ain't been too great between me and Sidney recently."

There's been a lot written and said about Nancy and sex over the years, mostly ignorant and derogatory. Young single woman enjoys sex – pre-AIDS, too – wow! Hold the front page! So if you're wanting any moral judgments or salacious details, you won't find them here.

Nancy was up first in the morning, getting dressed, fixed and making coffee before I woke up. She sat on the end of the bed, sharing a cigarette with me. Eventually, stubbing the fag out, she leant over, "Guess it's probably best all round if we keep that one to ourselves, right? No need to make things complicated."

Annie returned later the next day, followed in due course by Sid. "So what happened last night, then?" she asked almost straight away. I was wondering whether to own up, when I realised she was talking about my haircut, "I felt like a change and you're always moaning that my hair looks like Edna Everage or something. Anyway, I think Nancy did a really good job."

"Maybe I'll get used to it. Right now you look like a convict. Quite sexy though…"

I tried to avoid any subliminal meaningful glances with Nancy.

Sid returned in a foul mood, stamping round the room in his heavy boots and curtly dismissing anything Nancy asked him about the show or the rest of the group. Naturally I was paranoid that he'd sensed what had happened in his absence – though Nancy had assured me their relationship was open to other encounters. After a while they announced they were going uptown to the Glitterbest offices in the hope of persuading McLaren's PA, Sophie Richmond, to delve into the petty cash tin for them.

I was equally paranoid that Annie would suspect something, to the extent that I'd scoured the bed for any remaining traces of Nancy – especially her hair, given that there'd be no mistaking peroxide blonde from raven black. Soon though she was recounting the highlights of her Tufnell Park trip. Instead of the usual recital of Ella's latest put-downs, she told me of her conversation with Andrew, the owner of the house. Andrew wrote about films for a trendy little listings magazine, but regarded himself as even more of an authority on music. I wasn't so sure, given that he'd dismissed David Bowie as a lightweight no-hoper when I'd evangelised *Hunky Dory* a few years before, assuring me that Bowie would soon return to One Hit Wonder status. Normally he kept his distance where we were concerned, lest we jeopardise his burgeoning career and property-owning status with our marginal lives. This didn't preclude the occasional furtive request for us to get him some speed or cocaine, though. Generally, he'd carefully ration his vicarious contacts with our demi-monde. This had changed once he'd heard about our visitors. Andrew had undergone a miraculous overnight conversion to punk once it was clear that it wasn't going away any time soon. The old album collection was soon replaced by a gleaming new juke-box, packed with the latest 45s with the words "Singles are where it's at, man, who's got time for albums now?".

Since then he'd been angling for an invitation from Annie to come over and meet the others – just to hang out, of course. An interview with Sid would be a major exclusive for Andrew and no doubt make him a star on the North London dinner party circuit for months to come. So far we'd managed to put him off, but he'd decided that Annie could be the weak link, and I knew he'd be trying again.

"So he was telling me about how he'd had lunch with Richard Branson last week," she continued, "and how he'd been going on about what they were going to do with the Pistols … the album, and some big overseas tours…" It all seemed like some fairly harmless name-dropping until she said, "then Andrew said to him, 'That's all going to be a bit difficult with Sid's heroin habit, isn't it?' and Branson just freaked, you know? They were in an Italian restaurant in Notting Hill, really busy, and he was looking round in case anyone had heard. 'How on earth do you know about that! There's meant to be only two or three people…', so Andrew mentioned us." He'd then made Andrew promise to never repeat what he knew and assured him that the label would take a pastoral interest in getting help for Sid and protecting their investment.

She seemed rather pleased with this anecdote, and beamed at me when she'd finished, like how cool is it that we know more about what's going on than the hippest young capitalist in town. I was furious though. "For fuck's sake, Andrew has no right to be going round gossiping to people like that. Sid would go crazy if he found out. They'd feel really betrayed. Didn't you think of that? Tell him to fucking shut up next time – especially in public – and think a bit about what you say around him in future!"

Annie looked chastened, flushed angrily for a moment at the rebuke, started a half-hearted argument, but soon gave up. After a while an uneasy peace took over. I realised that the Tufnell Park story and the Branson drama had banished thoughts of Nancy the night before, and I'd navigated into safer waters. It was cool having the place to ourselves for the afternoon, safe in the knowledge that we'd be scoring later, as Sid never returned empty-handed from his cash missions.

For all the personal and emotional tensions that seemed to erupt more and more frequently between Annie and I, there were times when I'd look beyond the walls of the harsh and unforgiving environment we'd chosen. I'd remember what had brought us together to begin with, that sense of unique empathy and understanding between lovers, the all-night talking, finding someone at last who knew what you were on about, who wasn't going to laugh or trash you to their other mates. Sex and drugs had intensified the bonding, but it was ultimately down to good old fashioned love. For all the ugliness in our lives, there was still room for the occasional sunlit shaft of beauty or tenderness. And of course that was just where Sid and Nancy were at, those crazy us-against-the-world early days, although they'd have put it differently, I'm sure.

Suddenly I didn't want to be angry with her any more, and felt overwhelmed by affection. I'd got what I wanted, but at what price? She sensed my change of mood, and leant back on to my shoulder as I put my arm round her. It was so simple really. We didn't want to break that silent spell and return to the corruption and squalor of the everyday, but eventually Annie said, "Oh, did I tell you – I ran into Lucy and she said she'd be over this afternoon some time."

I rolled my eyes and bit my lip. It wasn't her fault, but Lucy was like the albatross in the *Rime of the Ancient Mariner* in terms of bad luck, and her visits always seemed to come laden with chaos and drama.

The Tale Of Lost Lucy

You know, some people got no choice
And they can't never find a voice
To talk with that they can even call their own
So the first thing that they see
That allows them the right to be
Why, they follow it, you know —
It's called Bad Luck

Lou Reed
'Street Hassle', 1978

Lucy was basically a sweet-natured kid from a well-off Home Counties family; small and elfin, with a rather pre-Raphaelite spirit and look. Flat sharing in Chelsea showed her a different world to the safe but dull life in Bishop's Stortford. She soon found the outré vibe of the King's Road dope scene more rewarding than her friends' endless quests for suitors and sports cars. On her good days she had a kind of insouciant, carefree quality that contrasted with most of her girlfriends' more hard-nosed approach to getting what they were after in the big city.

After a while she'd ingratiated herself with various boutique owners on the King's Road, most of whose shops seemed to incorporate at least one resident dealer, but in the end she was just another ingénue passing through, and failed to make any significant connections. The straight marriage market with the "old money" bachelors who abounded in Kensington wasn't for her either. Her diminishing status on the scene took an upturn when she hooked up with Alan, a stallholder from the so-called Antiques Market on

Kensington High Street. Not only did he have the cool Eagles look, but also access to more and better drugs than she was used to. Soon heavily-diluted party-girl cocaine was replaced by the deadly little greyish nuggets known as Chinese Rocks, as celebrated by the Heartbreakers, of course.

After the initial blast came comedown and tolerance, as weekend binges became daily needs. Soon it was necessary to sully her oh-so-delicate veins to get the desired effect, and she was forced to beat a retreat from safe havens like Lexham Gardens and Abingdon Villas and enter Alan's world.

Alan was a player, keeping her supplied with just enough dope to stop her looking elsewhere, but always maintaining the element of control to remind her who was in charge. But after a while she could no longer ignore the incessant gossip that pulsed round their local dope circuit of Alan's rip-offs, lies and scams. He'd operate mainly by "knocking" inexperienced dealers for gear on credit, hitting Lucy for cash if things came "on top" – she still had a job then – and resorting to outright theft and violence when she couldn't come up with the readies.

He'd been eager to please when we first met him with Lucy, but I soon learnt never to leave him unattended when they came round. Even so, he always seemed to be followed by little mysteries and disappearances – a tenner here, a deal or two there…

Lucy duly turned up, looking paler than usual. Annie routinely asked how she was doing, but reeled back in surprise as Lucy flung her arms round her, sobbing, "Oh Annie, it's all so shit … I don't know what to do, everything's so fucked up. And Alan…"

At this point it all became too much for her, burying her head in Annie's shoulder who looked across at me with a what-can-I-do raise of the eyebrows but Lucy rallied quickly enough and remembered why she was there.

Fumbling in her bag, she pulled out a couple of tenners. I couldn't help but notice the dull glint of a bracelet and some other jewellery before she closed it quickly.

"I can't handle going up to Michael's yet. Can you get enough for me to get straight, and I'll get more later?"

Reading between the lines, I suspected that she'd "borrowed" a few things from her mother's jewellery box but needed some chemical assistance before she haggled with Michael. I'd introduced them on her last visit, but as always she'd managed to attract trouble. Michael had been forewarned about Alan, and gave her little encouragement, "You just ask those nice folks downstairs to come up here, and if you've got the money then we're all happy but I don't want that fuckin' Alan around, okay?"

On her last visit she'd found that her bag had been dipped by one of the lads next in line. I'd noticed some furtive but hopeful glances being exchanged when they heard her refined tones. One of them quickly moved to sit beside her on the sofa, and did the whole "Hey, nice to meet you" distraction routine, while easing her bag into position. It all got way too complicated, with me having to negotiate the return of her property through Michael. I hoped things might go smoothly just this once, but it was not to be.

Once she'd got straight, Lucy relaxed a little, asked if there might be some more coffee and helped herself to another of Annie's fags, exhaling extravagantly. After a while she seemed more composed, and, sure of our attention, resumed her tale of woe. She and Alan had been kicked out of the flat she thought he owned. They'd moved between a series of squats, but as always accusations and Alan were rarely far apart and they'd had to move on again. Then they'd got busted. One of Alan's bail conditions required him to stay at his mum's place in Shepherd's Bush, while Lucy was exiled from London altogether, being banished to her parents' place in the country and having to sign on daily at the local police station, where her visits seemed to be the highlight of their otherwise soporific routine.

She'd started with good intentions, but London was still within reach, so drugs were never too far away. Anyway, her parents were in such denial about their daughter's shameful predicament that they'd readily accepted her story that it was all a silly mix-up about a little bit of cannabis. One night, though, she'd only just made it to the cop shop on time when John – the friendly young detective who always seemed to be around – waited till she'd signed on, before casually asking, "I'm sure I'm wasting my time, Lucy love, but what say I have a little look in your bag?"

She paled. How could she have been so stupid? Having a hit just before going to the police station, then shoving everything in her bag in case her mum had a snoop while she was out. But it was just an outfit and only the small remains of a £10 bag. She'd talked her way out of much worse things before. You get practice at that being around Alan, she thought ruefully.

"Oh dear Lucy, we seem to have ourselves a problem here," said John, indicating the contraband. John toyed with her like a cat with a mouse. He could keep it quiet. But there'd be a price – he'd want help, information particularly, otherwise his conscience wouldn't allow him to maintain her bail knowing that she was still committing offences.

She tried to explain that as nearly all the scoring was done by Alan, she could barely name a dealer to save her life, let alone the kind of major players John was wanting to collar. Of course he knew that too, but that was just the opening ploy. He reminded her of the risk he'd taken on her behalf, and now the time had come. However – luckily for her – there was another way she could repay John's favour... She had till the end of the week. Submit or risk loss of bail, a raid on her parents' house, and that would only be the beginning.

Now her sobbing was out of control. I was desperately trying to come up with anything consoling to say, or any practical way of thwarting the bent cop when I heard banging at the door upstairs. I was less than pleased to find Alan standing there and greeting me with exaggerated mateyness.

"Awright mate? Thought it'd look suss if I sat out there in the car much longer... Lucy done the business yet?"

I'd assumed she'd come on her own. Bloody great, I thought, having her dodgy rip-off boyfriend hanging around like a flashing "check this out" sign to any passing cop. I didn't buy the car story either – he'd probably been sitting on the wall outside, trying to clock who was coming to see Michael and which bell they rang so he could bypass me in future.

I was about to deliver my standard speech about Not Attracting Attention, but thought better of it. Much better just to get things done and send them on their way. I took her upstairs, where Michael revelled in stringing out the jewellery negotiations for as long as possible before sorting out her deal. Once back downstairs, I was looking forward to seeing them on their way once they'd had a hit. I glazed over and barely feigned interest in Alan's fake bonhomie as he gossiped away about mutual drug buddies. I heard footsteps on the stairs, and guessed Sid and Nancy were back.

But I wasn't ready for what happened next.

Violence

I was preparing to make introductions, when I saw
Lucy pale and step back with a little gasp as soon as
Sid and Nancy came in. Just as I was wondering if this
was some star-struck over-reaction, I saw Alan get up and
stride forward so that he was face-to-face with Sid. In a
moment the two men were snarling and swearing at each
other. Suddenly they were brawling, Sid's chains, padlock
and buckles clanking away as black leather fought against
blue denim. Then Nancy hurled herself into the fray,
raising the volume still further. Suddenly, in a brave but
ineffectual move, Lucy jumped up to Alan's aid, carefully
straightening her dress as she did so. Way out of her depth,
she tried to pull Nancy away by her hair. This foolhardy
move brought her a punch in the face from Nancy which
sent her staggering back across the room. Annie tried to put
a restraining hand on Nancy's shoulder, shouting at me as
she did so, "For fuck's sake, don't just sit there Denis – do
something!"

So far the fight was mostly playground grappling
sound and fury, the violence mostly verbal. But soon some
serious blows were landed, and I could see things escalating,
especially if they got to the kitchen with its ready supply
of knives and glass. I managed to get hold of Nancy's arm
and pull her away. She snarled at me as she overcame her
surprise, "Fuck off Denis, it's nothing to do with you."

"I don't give a fuck who you want to fight, just take it
somewhere else. I don't want it here!"

There was a second or two of confusion, which gave
me the chance to push myself between Sid and Alan. Great

move, I thought, they'll probably both batter me now. Alan stood with his back to the half-open door, so I placed a hand on his chest and pushed him back firmly.

"Okay – just fucking leave, Alan, you're well out of order… Lucy, get your stuff together. Sorry, you've got to go too – and don't bring him next time."

I noticed that Nancy and Annie had guided Sid over to their bed, where he sat red-faced, breathing heavily, and glaring menacingly at Alan. Nancy was still threatening and taunting Lucy, who trembled like a sparrow chick at the mercy of a cat. Somehow Annie and I managed to enforce a safe passage out of the place, guiding them up the stairs and out of the front door, Lucy having to tearfully pull Alan after her as he continued to curse and threaten, while Annie contained the others downstairs. Sadly that was the last we saw of Lucy before she was swallowed up by the junk underworld.

Sid was still bristling and hyper from the ruck, and directed an angry glare at me when I got back.

"You shouldn't have done that, you know? It was just between me and him, I was going to kill that cunt. I should have stabbed him last time, him and that stupid bitch!"

"I don't care. I don't give a shit if you want to fight Alan. But don't do it at my place…"

Nowadays it would all be framed in terms of "respect" and boundaries. Back then it was a simple matter of some seriously ignorant behaviour, and – middle-class and un-punk as it might sound – plain bad manners when they were staying in our place as guests. I was still annoyed by Sid's defiant attitude and the lack of any apology from either of them as I continued, "Look, I know that guy's scum and I don't like him any more than you do. How come you know him?"

Sid told his story with Nancy occasionally prompting him or filling in extra details. Not long after he'd joined Sex Pistols there had been a party in Chelsea. Everyone was having a good time, and they both laughed as they recalled the Chelsea débutantes, with their hair up and wearing their best frocks for "The Season", who'd dashed off to the Ladies' Room on hearing of the presence of Punk Royalty. A few moments later they'd all trooped back, with hair carefully mussed-up and bedraggled, and make-up anarchically smeared. One of those girls was Lucy, and that was how Alan came to be there.

After a few drinks Alan had started to feel out of place among the society girls and their suitors, and he didn't like the more alternative and outré arty types there either. Then he'd noticed Sid, recognising him from the recent frenzy of Pistols' stories and photos in the press. Soon his tabloid-fed mind was seething, and he started trying to wind Sid up, taunting him initially about the nickname, and then about punk in general. Who were these upstarts who hadn't paid their dues like the old guard rockers of Alan's day? Sid, for his part, had ruthlessly ridiculed Alan's shabby antique market fur coat and retro droopy moustache.

Eventually they'd taken it outside and a spectacular fight had taken place, turning into a running battle which culminated in a pure Errol Flynn moment, when Sid – on a landing halfway up an ornate staircase, had yanked a gilt mirror off the wall and smashed it over Alan's head as he charged up the stairs.

That was probably my first direct experience of Sid and violence. I'd heard and read many a story, of course, and there's no point dodging the issue with incidents like the assaults on Nick Kent and Bob Harris (presenter of *The Old Grey Whistle Test* show on BBC2. Famous – or notorious – for his description of the New York Dolls as "mock rock", and equally dismissive of the Pistols) – the attack on *NME* journalist Nick Kent being particularly brutal. Equally, there's no getting round The 100 Club incident, where Sid's attempt at hurling a beer glass at The Damned ended up with a woman being blinded in one eye. I'm trying as much as I can to only write about things I was directly involved in or witnessed at that time, or are known to have happened. Later I was to have a more personal experience when Sid was on his own territory, having had a drink or two, of how quickly his moods could change from joking around to potential violence with no warning or build-up.

All this was hard to equate with the Sid I knew most of the time: the thoughtful, witty guy, passionate about music and fiercely loyal to his friends. The real violence, though, was in Sid's head and in his past. It was there in the rage that would erupt most times when he talked about his childhood and his mother and for all the high-profile stories like The 100 Club, there were all the more private domestic episodes between him and Nancy which became more regular as time went on. These would often be followed by guilt-ridden reflections: self-hating and self-harm.

Holidays In The Sun

There's nothing more routine-centred than the eternal time-table imposed by drugs. After a while life settled into a familiar pattern. In the morning I'd go out for essential supplies. By the time I got back Sid would be arranging a meet or a pickup with the group's roadie-in-chief John Tiberi (a.k.a. Boogie), who seemed to be one of the few people he trusted in the growing entourage around the Pistols. Otherwise he'd summon the Glitterbest taxi and head uptown on his own. There would be the occasional good practice session, when Sid would come back buzzing and face a-glow. Generally, though, he'd return hours later, pissed off and cursing that no-one else had turned up or he'd been given the wrong information.

Initially we'd been naïve enough to hope that we'd get asked along some time – to "hang out with the band" in pre-punk parlance – although I could see this was unlikely, as not even Nancy accompanied him. One day Annie had been nagging me from the moment we woke up to ask if it'd be alright for us to go along today. I already knew what the answer would be, so didn't bother. She wasn't prepared to let it go, and snapped at me impatiently, "You always put everything off, don't you? If you don't say anything I'll ask him myself."

Mornings weren't the best time for any of us, so I made sure Sid was in a fairly good mood before accosting him as he came back from the kitchen with his coffee. I tried to catch his eye to convey "Hey, this isn't my idea", but only connected with squinty bleariness. He listened patiently to the request, while I noticed Nancy shuffling uncomfortably, then leaning forward alertly as she waited for his reply.

"No, I'm sorry Annie... there isn't really room there, and anyway – I, er, don't think you'd like it. The other guys take the piss and Malcolm doesn't want anyone else there. He's getting really paranoid about other people spying on us, you know? Anyway, most of the time I'm the only cunt who bothers to turn up..."

Annie took the rebuff with good grace, remembering all Sid's other trips uptown, when he'd return laden with bags of freebies, like the pre-release copies of 'Holidays in the Sun', plus masses of Pistols badges and t-shirts which we seized on readily.

Over time the little cracks of division and mistrust started to grow around and within the group. Sid would make his usual sullen return when a session had been aborted, but now he seemed even more pissed off on when the others did turn up. Factions were starting to form – to begin with Sid would complain that Paul Cook and Steve Jones were becoming yes-men who'd always obey McLaren. Soon though his discontent would focus much more on Johnny Rotten, or McLaren's perceived favourable treatment of the singer over the rest of the group.

To begin with it all seemed in part with Sid's general joking and sense of the absurd. The first series of complaints were inspired by Johnny's newly acquired taste for wearing hats. At first it was all a joke, as he'd poke fun at a beret and a wide-brimmed black matador number that he found particularly ridiculous. He found the whole hat thing effete and pretentious – "How can you take someone wearing a hat seriously?" he'd laugh. It was a theme he'd return to with some venom on 'My Way' the next year, but gradually the jokes would formulate into something more serious.

The intense friendship that had taken Sid and Johnny through their teen and college years and out into the nascent punk/squat scene was crumbling as events moved ever faster, with roles and loyalties changing overnight. Then there were the added factors of Sid's first all-consuming romantic relationship – a big enough deal in itself in the intense world of teen boy bonding, but raised a few levels more once Nancy was seen as the culprit for Sid's escalating drug use.

For her part, she bided her time. Soon though she'd join in, knowing that she'd be safe now in following Sid's lead and putting down John. There'd been a couple of times before where she'd overstepped the mark – once sneering at Rotten's choice of clothes and Catholic background, only for Sid to rapidly spring to his mate's defence. Gradually, though, she'd start to push a little harder, praising Sid, telling him that he was now the band's main attraction, along with constant digs about the management and the rest of the group, and moving carefully towards her main point – that Rotten had become that most dreaded thing, a "Sell Out" in his quest for frontman stardom.

One of her favourite anecdotes concerned a frantic search for Johnny after he'd disappeared mid-session. Eventually he'd been found, "hiding" allegedly, behind some amps and speakers, and most un-punk of all, he was reading a book, namely Graham Greene's *Brighton Rock* – an interesting choice.

But what really irked Nancy – as an avid reader herself – was that he'd copped out and said he'd only just picked it up because he was bored and it was shit anyway, when she knew that really he loved reading. After that he started to bring a bunch of mates and cronies along with him, and spend his time exclusively with them unless forced to deal with group business. By now Sid was feeling ousted from their friendship, sometimes resentful and angry, but just as often regretful.

"John's changed so much," he'd say, "he used to be a great bloke on his own and didn't give a fuck what anyone else thought – now it's like he's got to have this crowd there all the time to laugh at all his jokes, and go 'Oh you're so wonderful John'. It makes me sick…" He paused for a moment, "… and you know how I said I couldn't take you cos it would just start trouble with the others? It's totally different if he wants something – he's the big star now, you know, and he has to have his way or else…"

The 'Holidays in the Sun' single had been a big event, eagerly anticipated with everyone hoping for another searing blast like the mighty trio of preceding singles, 'Anarchy in the UK', 'Pretty Vacant' and 'God Save the Queen'. Excitement was high the day Sid and Nancy returned from one of their trips with carrier-bags full of advance promotional copies, t-shirts and badges. I looked at the sleeve as Sid proudly presented me with my copy. The Situationist influence hinted at on the earlier sleeves – such as the bus going to "Nowhere" – was more overt now, with the mainstream advert graphics subverted by altered speech bubbles. And of course it was the first Sex Pistols record since Sid had joined.

So the single pounded away on repeat. Annie even started dancing to it until Nancy said her bum was sticking out too much and that wasn't cool for punk rock. Over and over it played, Nancy acting as cheer-leader, stamping round the room shouting out the lyrics, while Sid crouched on the side of the bed, living every note of the music. His music.

Soon she'd decided that what really made the record great was her Sidney's bass-playing, miming the riffs passionately as she moved. I'm sure she'd be amused to know that all these years later, lovers and haters of the group still debate whether it's Sid, Steve Jones, Chris Spedding or a session man playing bass on that track. Equally, there were whispers – mainly from the camp who saw McLaren as a Svengali-like genius plotting the group's every move – that maybe the lyrics weren't entirely the work of Johnny Rotten, with nods in the direction of the group's art director, Jamie Reid, an old Situationist buddy of McLaren's. It was as if the basic premise of the lyrics – 'A Cheap Holiday in Other People's Misery' – would have been too subtle and subversive for the singer to come up with.

Those first three singles had all the power, energy and attitude, compressed into a few minutes of classic groups like The Who or the Small Faces but free of any self-conscious retro element. It made a perfect counter blast to the bland pop, disco and diluted doo-wop that dominated the charts. 'Holidays in the Sun' certainly had plenty going for it – like the stomping jackboots, a killer chorus, and the great alienated Rotten whine at the end, "Please don't be waiting for me" yet it was always going to be hard to deliver the same impact as earlier tracks, and this was the first moment of doubt for me. Annie and I agreed quietly that it was the least exciting Pistols single so far. Within a week or so it started to make its way towards the back of the record box. After the blowtorch rage and merciless accuracy of the earlier lyrics, complaints about the uncaring consumerism of the leisure industry seemed a bit tame. What would they do next? Protest about bin collections or public transport? There was something forced about the lyrics, which have always sounded to me like parts of two or three other songs put together. Compared to the concise and clever wordplay of the earlier singles, lines like "I don't wanna go to the new Belsen" seemed like a cheap shot at controversy or maybe hoping for another publicity-attracting BBC ban. Sid reckoned it was a reference to his old Flowers of Romance song, 'Belsen Was a Gas', and took it as a hopeful sign that it'd be recorded by the Pistols before too long.

Inevitably, given the differences in age and experience, it wasn't always "All for one and one for all" between the four of us. There'd be times when we'd disagree completely, like their "Spot the Nigger" game – sure, we knew they weren't really racist, and it was more about openly defying a taboo and shocking the "straights" – but with groups like the National Front rising to prominence, it just felt ignorant

to us. Probably in response to our liberal "Hey, what about
Civil Rights?" stance, they'd wait for the appearance of one
of the first young Asian women presenters on TV, and then
take it in turns trying to outdo each other in racially abusing
her. We'd sit there silently like disapproving parents.

Another time we got into an argument over the issue
of Nazi imagery and in particular the swastika which was
very prevalent on the punk scene. As expected, the defence
was that mainstream society needed shocking out of its
complacency, and if the swastika attracted more publicity,
of whatever sort, why not? Nancy – who was Jewish herself
– came out with something facile to the effect that sure,
the Nazis might have been bad but they had really cool
clothes and much better design sense than the Allies. Soon
Sid would joining in, extolling the virtues and great look of
the Gestapo's long leather coats and jackboots, and where
the best places to buy them were. At least we didn't get the
excuse about the swastika being an ancient sun symbol.

The tone of the discussion changed though when
Sid talked about his Belsen song, going through the lyrics.
I hadn't heard them before, apart from the opening line,
"Belsen was a gas, I heard the other day". The rest of the
song was about much more than the simple shock value I
was expecting. I remembered teenage hours spent reading
about the Holocaust, repulsed but drawn in, long before
I found out that I'm half-Jewish. The details are subtly
combined in the song, so the viewpoint shifts from the
victims to their families to the frontline killers, with the
central image of the postcards nailing the incongruous
mixture of leisure and murder – the "Banality of Evil" as
the author Hannah Arendt called it.

Season Of Mellow Mists

T he damper autumn nights crept up on us. Given the minimal natural light in the flat we didn't take much notice of the shortened daylight hours. Something that became impossible to ignore was Nancy's asthma, which hadn't been an issue till then. One afternoon when Sid was out she'd dozed off on their bed. Within minutes she was sleeping deeply, but there was nothing peaceful about it, as she wheezed heavily and painfully, accompanied by all kinds of very unhealthy sounds from her chest and throat. She shrugged it off when we asked her about it, with a story that it was something to do with when she'd been kicked out of a squat and on the street during her early days in London. This didn't really seem to make sense with an allergy, though. She also seemed to have a mental block about her inhalers, which she'd either lose or forget to renew. Maybe she was in denial, but after a few 999 calls or dramatic dashes to the Royal Free Hospital up the road it seemed more like a mixture of aggressive attention-seeking and a deeper-rooted wish to be the sick child who's been neglected and needed cosseting back to health. Ambulancemen would exchange glances, rolling their eyes, on the nights when she'd be in full "high maintenance" mode, insisting that they wait until she'd decided what to wear for the trip back to Accident and Emergency.

Although Nancy liked to take on the role of the hardened, battle-scarred survivor with Sid, treating him like a willing but naïve protégé in need of guidance and protection, the vulnerable little girl was never too far away. Sometimes I'd look over at her when she was reading intently, and her face would seem to have softened and be younger, away in her own world, back to those childhood days when your books and comics can transport you far away.

I'd been disappointed when it became clear that Annie had found allies in her liking for having the TV on almost non-stop in the background. This was what her parents did in the little kitchen where they spent most of their time. I guess it was a reassuring ritual for her, but at times the inanity of daytime chat shows and light entertainment would get on my nerves. I'd expected Sid and Nancy to be music all the way, every day, but they were just as happy to zone out in front of the set for hours, their eyes reflecting the flashes of changing colour from the screen. These were the days of just the three channels and early close-down so we'd end up watching some pretty desperate stuff, relieved only by Sid's running commentary of witticisms and obscenities.

One night we'd ended up watching a particularly dull documentary about a family in the US, but which Nancy was determined to see to the end. The screen showed the typical gleaming 1950's family kitchen, then closed in on the mistress of the house putting down a saucer of milk for the pet pussycat. I'd noticed before from the movements of her head that Misha took a passing interest in what happened on screen, but it had always seemed a pretty basic response to light and motion. Now, though, she stirred from Nancy's lap, suddenly alert. She slipped down on to the floor and made her way right up close to the television, looking up intently at the screen. Suddenly she reached up with her paw, first touching the virtual saucer of milk, then the other cat. Puzzled, she then made her way round to the back of the set, in the hope that the entrance to this feline other-world might be found there. She turned back towards us, thwarted, and let out a pitiful meow.

Nancy watched the whole performance with delight, and said, "Wow, that's amazing! She thinks there's another cat there. That's really intelligent, you know?"

Sid pointed out that it would have to be pretty small in that case, and we bantered on for a while, enjoying the sudden innocent pleasure of the moment. Soon Nancy was telling us how she'd never been allowed any pets as a child, in case they distracted her from her education, and in any case, her parents said animals were dirty and inconvenient and didn't really belong indoors. It was fascinating hearing this different, quite sentimental, side of her and it was good to know that she felt safe enough with us to open up without fear of being laughed at. Sensing the mellowness of our mood, Nancy – astute as ever – voiced out loud a whisper we'd picked up on a couple of times lately, in the form of discontented muttering about the confines of their single bed. Soon she was making her move, "Hey you guys, we've been sleeping in that fuckin' tiny little bed for ages now. You got so much room."

She indicated, stretching out luxuriantly on our bed. I wasn't too sure, sensing that this could be the thin end of the wedge but soon they were back in their double-act mode, Sid quickly backing her up, "Yeah, it's really uncomfortable. Nance nicks all the fucking blankets and I've got me arse freezin' up against the wall."

Annie and I looked at each other, uncertain, but Nancy wasn't about to let things drift, "Well, how about just for tonight, then? You have your bed back tomorrow, okay? Like, me and Sidney really need a good fuck…"

You might have wondered about the sexual logistics of two drugged-up couples living in the one room. Unconsciousness by one party or the other certainly helped, but in any case their sex life was almost non-existent, mainly due to Sid's narcotic intake. There'd be some snogging, baby talk and oral sex, but when it came to what Nancy really wanted, Sid was rarely able to rise to the occasion.

For our part, we found that the enforced closeness of the little bed had its advantages, especially for just the one night.

Alas our bed failed to make the earth move for them. After that there'd be the occasional chunter from Nancy about the single bed, but really it was another way of digging at Sid indirectly, and reminding him not to take it easy just because the new record was out. This would be the driving force behind their increasingly frequent arguments, whatever the spoken pretext.

The Autumn Cull

Even the most unrepentant addict would find it hard to deny that hard drugs and death are natural companions. So many of the people here didn't make it through, and many of them died way too young. Maybe they were consoled by the lines I heard many times from Sid and Nancy about "Live Fast, Die Young" but I doubt it. The deadly fatalism of those lame Beautiful Corpse clichés took no prisoners – but of course most of the casualties were mere foot soldiers in the drug wars, always destined for oblivion, unlike the star addicts.

But it does seem strange – given what was to happen later – that Sid and Nancy's time with us should have coincided with the most drastic conjunction of rock star deaths since the Brian Jones/Jimi Hendrix/Jim Morrison/Janis Joplin cull of 1969-71. In the space of a couple of months there'd be three significant tragedies, although some resonated with us more than others, it has to be said.

The first blow was struck on the night of August 16th. The night was still and stuffy when a late TV bulletin announced the death of Elvis Presley. There certainly weren't any comments at the time from Sid about Elvis's demise being overdue, and that his "fat paunch" had hung over rock 'n' roll for far too long (although elsewhere I've seen the alleged remarks attributed to Johnny Rotten). In fact I was surprised at how moved Sid was and by his respect for the man's music – in the earlier part of his career, at least. It was a revealing generational moment. Being five years older than Sid – almost a generation in teen-culture terms – I had too many memories from growing up in the long snooze of

the 1950s and its increasing subservience to the mindless
Cadillac and Coca-Cola American consumer culture. By
the time I was going to films and buying records Elvis stood
for everything corny and artificial, just as Led Zeppelin and
Pink Floyd filled the same role for Sid when he came to
the party. For me Elvis was never the riot-causing, proto-
punk, cop-baiting 'Pelvis' of the early years, who'd made
raw rock 'n' roll like 'Hound Dog' and 'Heartbreak Hotel'
but the emasculated GI who simpered his way through
pap like 'Crying in the Chapel' and 'Wooden Heart' (or
'Wooden Head' as my dad sneered whenever it came on the
radio). I could never see why we were supposed to worship
these remote idols with their Brylcreemed hair and preppy
clothes, and by the late Sixties he was a figure of fun for me
and my friends.

I'd noticed early on in their stay that the "Vive Le Rock"
t-shirt, with its classic Little Richard design, was one of Sid's
favourites, along with the two masturbating cowboys or the
leopard-print waistcoat. The Teddy Boy-ish red drape coat
with black reveres (usually worn with brothel creepers) was
another favourite. After a while I couldn't resist suggesting
mischievously that perhaps this was all a bit retro, possibly
un-punk, and all just a bit too American rock 'n' roll? Wasn't
punk about dynamiting mindless reverence for the past? In
Sid's view there was a real uncorrupted purity to Fifties rock
'n' roll, with its innate rebel spirit, which produced a brief
golden age of sharp, short, rebel music before the business
took over and sanitised everything for the mass audience.
This was the territory the Sex Pistols wanted to reclaim. It
was an idealistic vision, a romantic world of James Dean
lookalikes walking in off the street to cut an instant classic
at Sun Studios before disappearing into the hot Southern
night.

I hadn't expected him to be just as keen on the Elvis
of the 1968 TV comeback, or the 1973 *Aloha from Hawaii*
concert film, though. Here the appeal was more about

Elvis's appearance. Sid hated groups like Pink Floyd who were virtually indistinguishable from the road crew in their old jeans and t-shirts. If someone wanted to be a star or just expected people to pay to see them, the least they could do was to put on a show, and not look like they'd just come in from doing the gardening. In the 1968 show Elvis had slimmed down and reverted to his Fifties mean black-leather look, while the 1973 classic late phase Elvis look – the rhinestone-studded jumpsuit and the American eagle cape – earned Sid's respect for its sheer excess. There was also a real respect for the way Elvis defied all the superior critics who'd dismissed him as a corny has-been and made a return like the old champ who couldn't resist one last fight – even if he was overweight and with sweat messing up his pancaked make-up.

There was no ambivalence among us when Marc Bolan was killed exactly one month later. Whichever period of his life and music we each identified with, this was on a par with the deaths of major players like Jimi Hendrix or Jim Morrison earlier in the decade. To me, Marc Bolan and Tyrannosaurus Rex had been a huge part of my late Sixties teens, first as favourites on John Peel shows, along with the likes of Captain Beefheart and Country Joe and the Fish, and then as a regular at the early Hyde Park free concerts. By the time he'd become a chart-topping pop star in the early Seventies with T Rex I was in the grip of full-blown musical snobbery, deciding that he'd sold out, and anyway, he had none of the intellectual or artistic baggage of my hero and his rival, David Bowie. This of course was exactly the version of Bolan that Sid loved – the moves, the pout, the trashy glam outfits, and all the hits. I told him about my friend Chelita, who'd been married to Bolan's producer Tony Visconti. Whenever I went over there I'd always coveted the framed telegram on her toilet wall from Bowie to Bolan, written at the height of the music press driven "Glam Wars" which read "Darling, they're trying to start a war!"

Fate had added an extra wild card in placing the fatal
car crash at Barnes Common, close to where I'd grown
up and gone to school. Green and beautiful by day, the
common had a slightly scary and sinister vibe at night,
with its poorly lit and meandering paths through ominously
dark thickets. According to the more paranoid locals it was
simply a matter of whether the skinheads or the Satanists
got you first. I imagined the many tall trees and wondered
what had happened. Annie had been picking at her guitar
half-heartedly all evening, but had stopped playing while
we were talking about Marc Bolan. For once the place was
silent, until Sid spoke up, "Do you know any T Rex songs,
Annie?"

Before she could answer, Nancy butted in, "Yeah, you
know that one that Thunders does? 'The Wizard'? He
knows every fuckin' thing Bolan ever did." That was news
to me at the time, but she was quite right. There's a lot in
common in rock 'n' roll idealism between the two men, and
a similar obsession with looking sharp as well as sounding
good but I loved the way Johnny Thunders had defied
orthodoxy by going for one of the hippiest, trippiest songs
from the incense and patchouli days of Tyrannosaurus Rex.

Alas she didn't know that one, and attempts at doing
another early free concert favourite – 'Deborah' (who looked
like a "zeb-orah") – soon foundered. Annie asked Sid if he
could write down the chords as she worked them out, only
to get an apologetic shrug in return. If we'd been united
in our response and shared emotions when Bolan died,
the next fatalities were to produce no such finer feelings.
Five weeks later Southern rock and boogie outfit Lynyrd
Skynyrd were decimated in a plane crash. I'd never liked
the group, who sounded like a dumbed-down version of
the Allman Brothers to me. Even so, I was surprised by the
vehemence of Nancy's reaction and her callous disregard
for the victims, "Say, the plane probably went down cos that

singer's so fuckin' fat, you know?"

When late night TV decided to mark the occasion by playing the whole *Old Grey Whistle Test* version of 'Free Bird' she was barely able to contain herself. For once she was speechless. I could see she was almost physically repulsed at the sight of the group. She gestured towards the TV with distaste, as the lumbering singer lurched around between denim-clad long-haired guitarists, twiddling away into the distance. Every false ending provoked more ire. She couldn't get the words out quickly enough, but I knew exactly what she wanted to say: this simply embodied everything she hated in music in every way.

Half in love with easeful death, as Romantic poet John Keats observed, we were so casual with our own lives and so blasé about death as it crept around us. We could hardly be surprised at what was to follow.

Winter Nights

Soon winter came, dampness seeping from the walls as the cold tightened its grip on the house. After a while the flat was haunted by an inertia-inducing chill, as keeping warm almost overtook taking drugs as our main priority. People now often say "Wow, that must have been amazing" to me about our time with Sid and Nancy, but there were days when I'd look round the room at everyone in their familiar positions – Nancy hogging the music weeklies, although she could only read one at a time, Sid trying to work something out on the bass, Annie chain-smoking and fiddling around with her tobacco tins and paints – and feel stifled and want away from our close confinement. Solitude became a real luxury.

From time to time Nancy would nag Sid about when were they getting their own place, but the answer always seemed to be soon but not yet. With all the squats close by, there was no shortage of places to go for a cuppa and a joint but these trips would usually turn into a question and answer session about our visitors. Often I'd wander at random, sometimes to Hampstead Heath, or maybe browse in some bookshop or the local library.

A couple of years earlier I'd had a stall at the Golborne Road end of Portobello selling second-hand books and albums mostly, plus a few clothes and other odds and ends. It had been a good time, brought to a halt when Annie's car packed up, followed soon after by the arrival of the Singapore connection.

I'd sometimes end up meandering down that way, passing the Westway en route. Whenever Annie was pissed off it would be one of her favourite topics to berate me with, why didn't we start doing the stall again? But with no transport and hardly any stock the idea was a non-starter anyway. I'd go and check out our old corner spot, and usually have a chat with Jinty the pitchmaster. He'd ask when we'd be coming back and I'd say something vague but positive, but knowing different. It was always easy to kill some time in the Record and Tape Exchange further up Golborne Road – although our friend who'd managed the place had succumbed to his habit and moved on – before concluding with a last cuppa and a slice of toast in the caff where Pink Fairies frontman and counter-culture activist Mick Farren held court, recognisable from his perennial black Afro-style hair and black leather jacket. I'd been a big fan of the Underground press earlier in the decade and would have loved to have talked to him but an initial bad impression ruled that out. Farren was a huge amphetamine fan and loathed what he called the "death drugs" like heroin. He'd objected strongly one time when we'd sat at his table, only for Annie to nod out into her coffee. After that it would be the 28 or 31 bus home, and a return to the lockdown.

Nothing would seem to have happened at the flat in my absence. Everyone would be in pretty much the same places as before. Sometimes it felt like no-one had even registered that I'd been away. At other times, though, I could see there had been fervent speculation – had I maybe sneaked off to some secret private pleasure zone on my own? Sid could be quite snide then, making stage-whispered comments to Nancy about "selfish bastards". I'd realise that Annie was scrutinising my eyes to see if they betrayed any signs of indulgence, before hissing at me, "So, have you got something?" before turning away with a grunt when I said that I'd just wanted to get out and have some time to myself.

It wasn't the lack of "privacy" as such that got to me. If that had been the case, we wouldn't have got past the first week, but soon issues of bare flesh, bodily functions and sexual activity faded into the background. When we were alone, we'd wonder if Sid and Nancy's long-promised flat would ever materialise. For all the adventures and high times, we knew that we were in a kind of extended fantasy, and that at some time the painted bubble would burst and we'd be back where we were pre-Sid. Asking them directly was risky, implying that they weren't welcome, so we'd rely on the occasional details that came our way. But things were always nebulous and confused around the Pistols. The *Never Mind the Bollocks* album had come out, to predictable manufactured outrage in the mainstream media and some retail chains. There was talk of a possible US tour, some UK dates, and more and more hints at some kind of film.

By that time the Anti-Nancy Factions within the group, management and record label were getting restless, and serious efforts were planned to try to get her off the scene before committing to things like touring overseas or buying Sid a flat. At the end of November they moved out for a week to a hotel in Paddington, generating a series of wild tabloid fantasies of a drunken Sid dangling Nancy out of a window by her hair but there was nothing made up about the attempted kidnap while Sid was away in Holland with the group at the beginning of December, when a "dentist's appointment" – arranged for Nancy by certain members of the group's inner circle – turned into a one-way trip to Heathrow. If the idea was to present Sid with a *fait accompli* on his return – she's gone, end of story – they'd underestimated Nancy's feisty determination to protect her interests. I didn't get the full story from her until later, when it had been recounted and polished so many times that it had become more like a cartoon strip, with her righteously laying out all the haters whose sordid little plan she'd foiled.

Soon they were back – the hotel's lack of dealers hadn't helped – but confident this time that they'd soon be moving into a place of their own. Meanwhile the group was busy with a series of gigs here and in Holland. Word got round quickly one day when Sid came back from a trip to Virgin with a load of copies of the album and related freebies. Suddenly we had Michael and all his cronies lined up in our place and on their best behaviour as Sid dished out copies of the album. I managed to get hold of one with a "variant" green and purple cover that disappeared within a few days. We even had a state visit from Michael's main-man, Jimmy, who had acknowledged the occasion by adopting a more Tom Petty-ish restyling of his blond locks from the usual Rod Stewart look.

Jimmy fawned shamelessly as he waited his turn with Sid, who smiled quietly to himself when he declared, "I've got right into all that punk rock now Sid – you know, The Boomtown Rats, The Police…"

Even Gilly came back one time – bearing a whole pile of albums for signing. Sid laughed as he looked at them, "You opening a shop, then?"

The bonhomie generated by the album's release didn't last long. There was still time for one more confrontation. Tension had been building up between Sid and Michael for a while. The novelty of being able to show off one of the Sex Pistols to his customers had soon worn off for Michael, particularly once it became clear that Sid simply wanted to get his drugs – by any means necessary – and get the hell out of the place as soon as he could. He had no interest in being part of the "inner circle" who fawned around him late into the night. When Sid was coming back from Pistols' activity he'd often make a pit-stop upstairs before coming down to our place. A couple of times he'd been out of cash, and left his bass there as surety 'til the next day. I was surprised at Sid's laxity with his instrument, but he was confident that no-one would dare mistreat it. It was only a matter of time before the arrangement soured – Sid needed his Fender for a rehearsal, but it was early in the day, with an un-mellow Michael bluntly informing him, "No money, no bass".

I knew it was a bad sign when Sid came back minus guitar. He made a couple of brief phone-calls for backup, then rummaged through their many bags until he'd found what he wanted – a knife and a chain. Brushing aside Nancy's offer of help, he stomped back up the stairs. Annie and I looked at each other anxiously, knowing that things were spinning out of control and we were helpless to stop it. I could hear raised voices and doors slamming upstairs. I don't know what happened up there – I think it stopped just short of actual violence, but when Sid returned, clutching his bass and breathing heavily, he was soon followed by Michael invoking heavy IRA guys he claimed to know in Kilburn saying that this wasn't over. Sid seemed unimpressed and ignored him.

A couple of days later Michael made an unexpected appearance at our back door. I went to see what was up – maybe he'd locked himself out upstairs or Mary was too out of it to let him in? Once I opened the door I noticed someone standing behind Michael, dragging on a fag and looking around shiftily.

Michael made sure I was paying attention before turning to his mate, saying, "This is where you'll find that cunt Sid".

Not that Sid was in the least bothered, dismissing Michael's threats with a sarcastic guffaw, "Oh, I'm so-oo scared," he laughed.

Although Sid played it cool, there was no doubt that he was very proud of the album. Here was the validation of his dreams, and proof of the strange and unpredictable events that had taken him from the West London squat scene to global fame. There have been whispers ever since as to Sid's actual involvement in the recording and playing of the album. None of this mattered to Nancy, though. For her the album proved what she had been saying for weeks by then, that Sid was the true spirit of the group, while Rotten was running out of ideas and credibility. She'd go on to claim that Sid had written most of 'Bodies' and 'Submission' and try to goad him into being annoyed that his 'Belsen was a Gas' hadn't made the final selection.

We couldn't help thinking that there was an inescapable feeling of looking back about the album, with all the Pistols' four singles there, and not much that hadn't been heard before. While the group and management had been going through all the high-publicity contract dramas with EMI, A&M and Virgin, the majority of their nearest UK rivals – The Clash, The Jam, The Damned and The Stranglers – had got their albums out months before and were looking ahead. Now the pioneers seemed to be playing catch-up. In the same way, the sharp and distinctive style in the group's artwork and graphics – the collages, the kidnap lettering – had been a vital part of the Pistols' impact and status as leaders of the punk pack but it had soon been absorbed into just another marketing gimmick for the record labels. The badges, record sleeves, posters and clothes had laid out a ground plan away from the usual rock career path, but now everyone had them. I knew I'd be in the minority, but I thought the album title was crude and oafish, and looked like a lowest-common-denominator attempt at garnering some free publicity when the tabloids seethed and the retail store bans started to pile up. For the first time it felt like the group were keeping pace with the scene rather than leading it. Sid didn't think my view even merited a reply, and just snorted derisively. Still, it was entertaining trying to explain the many usages of the word "bollocks" to Nancy.

"Shit, they won't have a clue what it's about in the States," she sighed.

Among the supplicants was Gerry, the underling of Michael's who had unwittingly brought about my meeting with Sid and Nancy earlier that summer. Nancy rolled her eyes at us as he made his entry. After he'd wheedled a copy of the album from Sid, the real reason for his visit became clear as he reached inside his denim jacket and pulled out a small bag. "I remember you used to like these – the old morphine jacks. Some people do 'em £3 a throw, but I'll do you a hundred for £150, and I'll lay them on as I know I can trust you."

The little soluble morphine tablets – allegedly East German army surplus – had appeared the previous summer and were useful if smack or money were in short supply. The pills certainly punched their weight: although morphine isn't as strong as heroin, the tablets gave a serious rush when hit up, producing a hot surge followed by an intense burst of pins and needles that jangled everything from your spinal cord to your brain stem and all points in between. I considered Gerry's offer. It was a good deal, but I didn't want that many. There was plenty of H about, and I couldn't see the weaker tablets selling. I was starting to let him down gently when Nancy butted in, "Hey, we'll go halves with you. Fucking-A, man, that's a good price!"

Once Gerry had left we divided the tabs up between us. My standard dose had usually been three, but decided to celebrate with five, Annie and Nancy following suit. Sid seemed to have been over at the table for ages, and once my rush had eased, I called over to see what was happening.

"Fucking bastards take all day to fucking dissolve," he cursed.

"Yeah, they're a bit slow at first, but once the water's hot enough they're gone," I replied and went over to see if I could help. Sid was stirring at a grey jelly-like mass in the spoon with growing annoyance. I fetched some more water and gave it to him.

"How many have you got there?" I asked.

He frowned and gave me an angry squinty look like it was a really stupid question, "All of them –what do you think?"

I was startled and immediately a tabloid headline flashed through my head, "Punk Rock Star ODs in Eton

Avenue Squat".

"I don't think that's a good idea. Do a few to begin with and see how it goes," I advised.

"Fuck off, I want to fucking feel something!"

I looked at Nancy for support, but she gave me a little shrug and went back to watching the TV.

I kept a discreet eye on Sid as he shot up a few minutes later. There was an involuntary exclamation of "Shit!" as the gear hit, and he slumped forward, head between his knees and the needle still hanging from his arm.

Nancy called out, "Hey, you alright?" – no answer – then, "Sid quit fucking about, what's up?"

"Fuck sake, can't I enjoy a rush for like two seconds without you on my case," he replied wearily after a tense pause, raising his head as he spoke, Nancy shrieked, "Oh Sid, what's happened to your face?"

I looked across, and sure enough a transformation worthy of Mr Hyde was taking place. His face had first gone a beetroot colour – remarkable enough, given his usual pallor – and was now turning into a mass of mottled lumps, bumps and blotches. He lurched over to the mirror by our bed, took a look, and reeled back laughing, "Fuckin' 'ell Nance, I'm turning into Frankenstein!"

"It's not funny, Sidney – what if you stay looking that way?"

This amused him even more.

"McLaren would fucking love it, I know that … Piss Rotten right off too…"

Soon though the excess colour faded, the rush and the buzz subsided, and Sid was on everyone's case, "Hey, if you aren't taking those pills, can I have 'em?". As if he was going to feel anything else after that dose!

We sat around joking about Sid's brief transformation and adapted the fantasy tabloid headlines to Punk Rock Facial Mutation Shock Horror.

December saw a return to live action for the group, and Sid's mood improved considerably once he was back doing what was most important to him. He was especially excited about the matinee shows on some of the UK gigs, and the chance to hang out with the Pistols' youngest fans. This put Nancy in an awkward position. She was genuinely delighted and excited for him, but the kidnap attempt had removed any hopes she might have had of being ultimately accepted into the Pistols' camp. Her presence was tolerated at a couple of the shows, but from now on Sid would feel increasingly under pressure and torn between rival demands.

Nevertheless Sid was insistent that we should come along to one of the Uxbridge shows, the nearest they were playing to London, and got together with Boogie to make sure we were on the guest list. I was excited about the gig, and couldn't understand why Annie was in such a grouchy mood. A series of explanations followed ranging from a migraine to other vague ailments, all rounded off with a prolonged and angst-ridden session of "getting ready" – clothes and drugs – and double-binds about various problems we might encounter in unfamiliar territory out there in the night. I started to feel a growing sense of dread – this isn't going to happen, we aren't going to make it – as departure time got pushed further back. Matters were settled finally when she fell into a deep heavy-breathing sleep. And that's what happened to my last chance of seeing Sex Pistols play live…

This was to be the start of a new and depressing phase where Annie, having taken not enough gear or too much, put an everyday blanket ban on doing anything beyond subsisting indoors. At last though there was progress on the accommodation front. Sensing that the tabloid vultures were hovering for the next round of lurid hotel stories, management and record label moved into gear and all obstacles were swept aside and a permanent place was bought. In no time at all Sid and Nancy moved into a flat close to the Westway and Warwick Avenue, at last leaving behind the days of rock star with "no fixed abode".

"Hey, you must come and see us when it's all fixed up, just give us a call," Nancy croaked as she struggled up the narrow stairs with the last of their bin liners and carrier-bags.

New Year

Nineteen seventy-seven might not have brought the "sten guns in W11" promised by The Clash, but it had been an intense and fascinating time, both in general and personally. It was hard to look forward too far in wondering what would happen next.

1978 started with the Pistols' US tour, an exercise in chaos that trailed the group through an exhausting cross-country schedule. Night after night we'd watch the news for the latest pictures of an increasingly strung-out and nihilistic Sid as he battled his way through the shows, looking more blood-stained and punch-drunk every time. There'd be further grim updates on the spectacle in the weekly music papers. We'd feared just such an outcome and could only look on helplessly. Any ideas that we'd had of the group turning into some kind of Rolling Stones like ongoing operation, where we'd find some form of suitably subversive employment, were soon forgotten.

Annie soon decided that life was dull without our punk rock star flatmates, and became increasingly irritable, depressed and lethargic. The Uxbridge episode had been a foretaste of what was to come. With Sid's taxi account no longer on call and our car permanently off the road, our world shrunk back to a small island round our bed, the TV and stereo, a path to the front door, and the narrow well-worn track down to the chemist by the Chalk Farm tube station.

She'd even manage to ignore Misha's early morning assaults on our toes (or any other protruding flesh) as we lay in bed. I'd get up to attend to the cat's needs, while Annie would burrow down deeper into the duvet, piling it over her like an igloo. On my return she'd either feign deep sleep, or snarl at me for disturbing her, "Thanks, now I've got to take my fucking methadone early" as she leant over to scrabble for one of my cigarettes.

Our waking time became a monotonous battlefield of arguments, resentment and prolonged tense silences, broken up by occasional explosions of tears, shouting or breakages from Annie. Visitors became a rarity. Where Annie seemed content to spend the days huddled in bed, chain-smoking and watching any old rubbish on TV, I'd soon feel caged in. Life became an endless double bind of insoluble and overlapping problems. She decided that she didn't like the flat any more adding hadn't I noticed that she'd never liked it!

Just being there was depressing but going out anywhere was too much trouble. Anything I said or suggested would be instantly trampled into the dirt, so I'd go out just to avoid another row. Then I'd be in more trouble for leaving her by herself.

Pindock Mews

One of Nancy's last actions before leaving had been to give me a hastily scrawled scrap of paper with their new address. I'd never heard of Pindock Mews. It certainly sounded an incongruously genteel address for them. Nancy assured me it was near Warwick Avenue tube station and would be easy to find. I'd been eager to go round and realised that it was now a fair while since they'd moved out of our place. I'd hoped a joint outing would lift Annie's spirits, but after a couple of attempted trips petered out in the glare of afternoon game-show TV, I decided I'd go alone.

Nancy sounded really pleased when I rang, much more positive and "up" than usual, bursting with things to tell me, and insistent we should both go over as soon as possible to hear all about the US tour and what was happening next with her and Sid.

I knew the area pretty well from living in Queens Park a few years before. It was a strange mixture of the affluent and the down-at-heel, with just as many squatted crumbling old houses as Camden Town or Hampstead. It wasn't hard to find once I'd stepped off the bus and got my bearings. I was struck first by the picture postcard look of the Mews – "Spring time in London" or some such – all hanging baskets and cobblestones, with a few expensive but discreetly parked cars and tasteful tubs of flowers. I felt self-conscious and out of place as I walked along trying to find their place, while not making it too obvious that I hadn't been there before.

The little traffic-free street was unusually quiet for that

part of town at that time of day. The rows of little cottages –
originally built as stables for horses with living space for the
grooms and livery men upstairs – generally had a slightly
fussy prettiness about them, while some of the downstairs
garages had been converted into more living space. There
was one working garage, doors flung wide open, while a
couple of blokes in oily overalls tended to a car inside. This
turned out to be downstairs from where Sid and Nancy had
the upstairs flat.

I rang the bell and waited, aware of being checked out
by the garage blokes as I stood there. I'd spoken to Nancy
on the phone, she'd said they'd be in for sure. I rang the
bell again, afraid that in a moment I'd have to slope off,
forgotten. Then, above the clang and screech of the garage
workshop, I heard a familiar voice calling from above, "Hey
who is it? Anybody there?"

Nancy leant out of the window, and let me in a moment
later. She led me up the narrow stairs into the hall. She
breathlessly indicated various rooms with a wave of the
hand, and I could tell straight away that this was possibly
the happiest I'd seen her. I could see that this was a real
moment of vindication for her. Here she was, despite what
all the haters and doubters had said, she was still with Sid,
and now they were on the first upward step with their own
place together.

She led me into the front room overlooking the
mews. We sat down on the white L-shaped leather settee
that dominated the room, I smiled inwardly as I recalled
the times they'd come round with bundles of cash they'd
extracted on the pretext of "buying a settee". I noticed that
there was quite a strong smell of weed in the room, soon
accompanied by a suitable soundtrack, as she put on what
was to be the ruling sound of the day, the 12" version of Dr
Alimantado's 'Reason for Living'. That afternoon is one of
my favourite memories of that time, a tantalisingly brief
interlude of optimism and near-normality, where it seemed

that just maybe it could all work out. By the end of the day we were all harmonising (well at least making vocal noises at the same time) to the timeless plea, "Don't dee-termine my lii-iife".

Sid was still asleep, apparently, although I was sure I could hear the faint chatter of the TV from behind the bedroom door. Nancy led me into the small and cluttered kitchen. I managed to extract a couple of mugs from the washing-up piled in the sink, while she got the kettle going. It was a strangely normal domestic moment as we went about our tasks, chatting away as we wove around each other in the galley-like space. I opened the fridge door to get the milk, but the only bottles I could see were Pils and methadone, along with some milk shakes and cans of Coke. Nancy shook her head, in a "You just can't get the staff these days" kind of way. I was just about to say I'd have my coffee black, no problem, when she said, "Look, d'you mind going down to the shop? The one on the corner at the end of the road, y'know? At least you won't get fucking people jumping out taking your picture?"

Be careful what you wish for, as they say…

When I got back, Sid had emerged and was slouched on the settee, hair mussed up all over the place and cradling a spliff in one hand and a can of Fanta in the other. I'd wondered what sort of state he'd would be in – mentally and physically – after the nightmares of the American tour and the messy disintegration of the Pistols after the last show in San Francisco. He still sported a substantial bandage on one arm, but was in great spirits otherwise and even had some colour in his face. It felt like the early days at my place, as one story after another tumbled out, interrupted by many jokes and asides, with much laughter and the occasional pause for reflection.

I heard of the Methadone Disaster at Heathrow when Sid, drunk and stoned for the endless Atlantic crossing, had managed to drop his bag and shatter the precious bottle that was meant to nurse him through the month-long tour. That story was topped breathlessly as Nancy told me how she'd flown out to Colorado with emergency supplies, but had been unable to get past customs, "Shit, I wanted it to be like in the movies, you know? When the US Cavalry comes over the hill…"

At times it all seemed to merge into one big, mad adventure as they took it in turns to recount everything that had gone down since we'd last met. Sometimes they'd talk over each other in their eagerness to get to the best bits. I was eagerly waiting for Sid's account of the break-up and any news on what might happen next. I was surprised though when he broke off to ask me, "How come you're on your own then? Didn't Annie want to come too?"

Sid had been really friendly all along, and seemed genuinely pleased to have the three of us together, but there was a definite edge to his voice. I remembered his grouchy comments before when I'd needed space from the flat. I reminded him what had happened with the Uxbridge gig, and how that had been the start of the current phase where Annie could rarely be bothered to stir herself from the flat.

There had been a general upturn in their situation apart from getting the flat. A suitably discreet private doctor had been found to dispense large amounts of methadone to them both. Money was readily available most of the time now that Sid represented McLaren's last possible asset. There was naturally still ongoing Sex Pistols business despite the end of the group – mainly the film project, *Who Killed Bambi?* – which required dealing with the old regime. They were looking ahead in different directions, though. Nancy told me that from now on she was Sid's manager, as that way they could both finally be sure of not being ripped off. I looked over at Sid, who nodded in agreement. While I was pondering on that, she continued that the next step would be a move to New York. She reckoned she knew the scene there as well as anyone, and had the contacts with the kind of clubs and promoters they'd need to deal with, as well as trump cards like her knowing top photographer Bob Gruen. And of course she had the other "connections" that they'd need there. She and Sid were convinced that London's brief moment as the epicentre of the punk scene had been and gone, and the "Big Apple" was where it was at. Sid was keen too, and reckoned that once in New York he'd get together with Heartbreakers Jerry Nolan and Johnny Thunders to form punk's answer to Blind Faith. They'd already played a few gigs together in London and Sid thought they'd been great. It seemed like a huge step. I'd loved New York when I'd been there for its energy and twenty-four hour action, but knew how the place could crush and spit out the weak and unwary.

Before I could get too deep into serious thought, Nancy came out with a series of hilarious and rude stories involving Russ Meyer, one of the prospective directors for the film. Meyer, known best for his garish sexploitation movies like *Beyond the Valley of the Dolls* and *Supervixens,* seemed a fair choice for the trashy but subversive McLaren aesthetic. He was also well-known for a mammary fixation demonstrated in his films, and this was something Nancy loved to exploit. She'd acquired a wide range of provocative undies from the Soho sex and fetish shops specifically for their meetings with the lascivious director and delighted in making him sweat and squirm as they talked. They'd been filming in Paris as well, and the French trip confirmed the post-Rotten balance of power. She'd loved that trip and the potential new direction towards films. I'd noticed before that Nancy was a bit of a movie buff on the quiet, and I sometimes thought she was discreetly trying to expand Sid's cinematic horizons beyond *Taxi Driver* and *Texas Chain Saw Massacre* (admittedly a favourite of hers too – they seemed to know the film by heart between them).

The room was filled with spring sunshine. Nancy sat by the record player, going through a stack of Virgin Front

Line roots reggae freebies, coming back time and time again to 'Born for a Purpose' but soon enough Sid took over, bursting with boyish excitement as he put on his 'My Way' single, before presenting me with my own advance copy. It was a poignant and positive moment, and as a kind of vindication for all the times I'd seen him return despondent from another cancelled group practice.

Sid took a real pride in the record, and relished the story of filming the video where he ends up shooting the audience. He wanted to be sure that I'd taken in his changes to the lyrics, which he was really pleased with. He went through the song line by line, delighted that I remembered the origins of "the prat who wears a hat" theme from the previous winter at my place, when the fall-out with Rotten had begun.

I'd wondered what kind of scene I'd encounter there on the bus journey down. I'd expected chaos and masses of elite punks coming and going. I certainly hadn't anticipated the almost tranquil domesticity I found. I didn't want to overstay my welcome though. I went back on the bus with Dr Alimantado's chorus to 'Reason for Living' pounding through my head, and the 'My Way' pre-release clutched tight to my side. It had been the best afternoon in ages. I tried to stay upbeat as I made my way down the stairs to the flat, hearing the familiar crackle of the TV from below.

I put 'My Way' on the stereo as I excitedly recounted the afternoon's events. Eventually Annie looked up and grumbled, "I wish I'd been there". I reminded her whose decision it had been to stay home. "You should've made me go with you!" she insisted.

Too much or not enough, it was all part of the pattern for the following months when the good times would rapidly fade into the past.

Eton Avenue Endgame

We watched from a distance as 'My Way' came out and made its way up the charts, and followed the increasingly tangled story of the film as Russ Meyer departed mid-shoot, and the project morphed from *Who Killed Bambi?* into *The Great Rock 'n' Roll Swindle*. Somewhere along the line we'd acquired a lodger, Barry, an older American doper who'd pitched up in Camden. I never liked or trusted him, but he was quick to exploit our transport neediness with his car. Soon he seemed to be around nearly all the time, affable enough but a bit too eager to please. Next he spotted that the bathroom was little used since the boiler had packed up, and in no time he'd got a mattress and installed himself there.

I'd confided in Annie that there was something about Barry that didn't ring true, and pointed out a few little doubts and inconsistencies in things he'd said and done. She dismissed this as male territorial nonsense on my part – a difference which he was quick to detect and exploit.

However, while he established his cuckoo-like presence at our place, things were about to change. For most of the time since Sid and Nancy left we'd been barely scraping by but one phone call was to change all that. The Singapore Connection guys were in town again and wanted to get back to work. This time, though, instead of the near-lethal, Heartbreakers approved "Chinese Rocks" brand, they'd brought some White Thai. I called Sid and Nancy and said that it'd be a good time to come round, adding casually that it was nothing to do with Michael.

They turned up a few days later on a bright Saturday

afternoon, preferring this time to come round the back way through the garden. Nancy hurried in, nose wrinkled in distaste, "Hey, did you guys know you've got a dead hippy in your back garden?" she sneered.

"He looks really rank," added Sid.

On a previous visit Sid had decided to slip out the back way, only to trip over the unconscious form of Kris, a visitor from the night before. Sid had come back in, telling me, "I think you'd better see this. There's some bloke passed out in the bushes. I think he's still alive but I'm not sure".

That certainly got our attention. Fearing the worst, I told Annie to stay indoors and start clearing up. Sid and I went back outside. Sure enough, Kris lay among the leaf litter, his face paper white. Evidently he'd stopped for a wee on the way out before being overcome and keeling over with prick still in hand.

This time the culprit was Barry. I didn't want him attracting unwelcome attention by sprawling around outside off his face and went to fetch him. No-one took much notice when we came back in – until Barry spoke. I could sense Nancy's hackles rising the moment she heard the American accent. That seemed to offend her even more than his ersatz David Crosby look of stringy untended hair and droopy moustache. Soon Barry was trying to show off, name-dropping people he claimed to know at Rough Trade records. He'd shown little interest in music before, and I was sure he'd come unstuck any minute.

I could see that Sid didn't think Barry even merited the effort of a put-down, but once he'd started to relate how Journey were "totally bitchin'" live, Nancy could restrain herself no longer, "That's just dinosaur shit, ma-aan", she said, emphasising the last word 'Pretty Vacant' style, "I bet you never even heard of the Dolls or the Pistols. Anyway, like, what the fuck are you doing here?"

I always found it amusing that Nancy, for all her "outside of society" hardcore stance, was so offended when

Americans let the side down, as it were, whether it was Barry or boogie merchants like Lynyrd Skynyrd. Barry stood for too many of the things she didn't like, and now he'd pissed her off even more by claiming a kind of common cause with her as Addicted Americans Abroad. He quickly sized up the situation, realising that he was out of his depth, and slunk off to the bathroom.

Nancy exhaled loudly and relaxed once he'd left us. She'd been holding her bag close to her all the while, but now opened it to reveal a sizeable heap of cash, informing me that once again the record label had stumped up for more fixtures and fittings at the flat.

"Hey, we got a bed, we got a TV, fridge … don't need much more than that. So whatcha got then?"

Sid sprang into life as soon as I got the bag out, but then looked suspiciously at the fine white powder as I tipped some out.

"Is that all you've got? The white stuff? You sure this hasn't been cut?" I assured him not, "Is it any good?" I assented, "So how d'you know then?"

I'd noticed that Sid had become a bit obsessive about being ripped off by dealers since moving out, and felt resentful at being put under the same suspicion. Still, I knew it was high quality gear and suggested there was one way to find out. Since the morphine mutation a while back, nothing about Sid's intake was likely to surprise me. I watched as he tipped a whole gram packet into his spoon and prepared it – until I realised from Nancy's frown that it was all for him. Sid hit up, shuddered, and looked round with a quizzical squint, before gasping, "Fucking hell mate, that's amazing – I've got to feel that again".

There was a kind of innocent, up-for-it "I just wanna get high" element to Sid as always, but as I doled out gram after gram, with diminishing financial returns each time. He'd developed a cynical "Only mugs pay for drugs" attitude, basically "Here's the money, gimme the drugs and fuck off" which didn't feel part of being mates, and definitely hadn't been there before.

Next time he came alone, turning up early and unannounced, leaving the Glitterbest taxi waiting outside. I told him I was in the middle of sorting things out and would call later, but he'd be welcome to stay for a coffee. Sid looked at me, before snapping, "Fuck it, I want something now – you're a dealer aren't you? I thought dealers were supposed to have fucking drugs, you know?" before clattering up the stairs and away, punk accessories all a-jangle.

In the end the wretched Barry became over-confident, and over-reached himself, just as I baited a trap that would finally confirm my suspicions of his stealing from the stash. I still had to call in physical assistance to eject him from the place, whining, begging and pleading. I'd hoped that this would be a kind of purifying act and removal of negative energy that would help Annie and I get our love and lives back together. Barry had seemed like the embodiment of everything bad on the dope scene, and a kind of warning from the future, lest we ended up the same way. The violent nature of his departure instead unleashed an atmosphere of resentment and mistrust. I tried to suppress the thoughts, but I couldn't help but see that Annie had probably been in league with Barry in his scheming and stealing. Even once he'd gone, he still seemed able to reach out into our lives and cause trouble. He claimed he'd been seriously assaulted at the flat, which meant police coming round for statements. Then he got caught robbing some other friends, and only had the gall to give our address in a vain hope of getting bail.

Annie meanwhile reminded me more and more of some voracious cuckoo in her appetite for drugs, and her increasingly casual attitude to how they were obtained. The bond of "Us Against the World" that had seen us through cold winters and many a crisis had gone for good. Now she was the one who'd disappear for hours, returning in

variously stoned states and treating me with a cold "You
still here?" indifference. Now I was no longer keeping her
in the style she'd grown accustomed to there seemed to be
nothing left, apart from a miserable daily round of sniping
and scoring points off each other.

Following another day and another argument, I knew
I'd had enough. We were meant to be going to her parents'
place in Brighton for a few days. We bitched and sniped
all the way down on the bus to Victoria station. She didn't
miss a nagging beat as we made our way towards the train.
I couldn't remember the last time we'd laughed together.
I knew that somewhere I still loved her but sadly 'All You
Need is Love' doesn't work when the chemistry between us
simply brought out the worst in each other.

Everything felt very clear suddenly. I stopped, and said,
"I don't need this. There's no point me coming with you".

I could see she hadn't expected that. For a moment
she was silent, before mustering all the bitterness she could
manage, "Well don't expect me to come back then".

At first she stormed off, but then she'd slowed down in
the expectation that I'd come running after her.

Not this time.

A few days later she was back, but by then we knew
there was no way we could carry on. A smashed window
in the kitchen and a glass of water contemptuously thrown
in my face were the last acts at Eton Avenue. "This is my
place, it shouldn't be me, but I'm going," I told her – not
knowing just how final that moment was to be – not sure
where, even, until I was heading down the road to the phone
box. Nancy sounded calm and relaxed when she answered.
I told her what had happened and asked if I could crash
there, "You guys fighting? Hey, that's shit, I'm sorry. Yeah
yeah course you can. Me and Sidney aren't doing anything,
see you later."

Pindock Blues

It was dark by the time I got to their place. We sat around listening to the usual reggae and Ramones background as I recounted all the recent bad news and upheavals. Nancy was very upbeat and positive as she had been earlier in the year when I'd visited. Whether she was really "managing" Sid or not, she was clearly excited about their impending departure for New York, and certain that he'd find the right people to play with and an appreciative audience. As the Pistols had bypassed the city on the US tour, she was adamant that people would go crazy to see Sid. Maybe he'd start off playing the punk clubs, but it was only a matter of time before he'd be the talk of the town.

However Sid seemed quieter and off in his own space a lot of the time. Eventually I asked if I could stay for a week or so until I'd found somewhere to live or resolved things with Annie. Nancy was sympathetic, "That's such a shame. She's great, Annie. Maybe you can sort things out?" – I shook my head – "No? Still you don't know – maybe in a while," then, almost as an afterthought, "Hey, it's okay if he stays isn't it Sid?"

He nodded in agreement, picked up his beer and went to watch television in the bedroom. We carried on talking for a while before Nancy turned in, leaving me to stretch out on the white leather sofa, listening to the unfamiliar sounds of the Paddington night as I vainly sought some sleep.

Generally things seemed much the same as when I'd last gone round there in the spring. As McLaren's remaining post-Pistols trump card, Sid was better paid than ever. The private prescription was still in place, along with a wardrobe full of surplus methadone. This would stave off any crises or dramas that would get unwelcome press coverage – but their drug of choice was still heroin. Sid would often be summoned away by taxi for Pistols-related business, leaving Nancy and I to pass the time together. Sometimes she'd get out her personal box of treasures, all the stuff that had somehow stayed with her through all the mad adventures that had taken her from the New York punk/junk underworld to this smart flat, with its discreet location and stylish decor. I'd seen the photo album before at Eton Avenue, along with the crumpled cutting of her review of the Heartbreakers from *New York Rocker* in 1976. One afternoon we were involved in yet another deep textual analysis of the songs from *L.A.M.F.*, with Nancy painstakingly moving the stylus back and forth to show that the chorus of 'Born To Lose' sometimes shifted to 'Born Too Loose', and explaining the significance thereof – when she jumped up and dashed out, returning a moment later clutching a small jewellery box, worn and battered round the edges. Handing it over, she simply said, "Look".

I opened the little box, not sure what I'd find beneath the cotton wool. It was a small black badge in the shape of a heart, no lettering, just a plain but stylish shape. At first I wondered if it was jet, but realised it was metal when Nancy took it out and held it against her shirt.

"See? If you wear this on a black background people can't really see it" – I wondered why, until she continued – "The Heartbreakers had like, fuckin' fifty of these made – really early on you know, when Richard was still there – and only gave them to people they were really close with. So if you were in a bar or someplace, and you saw someone with the black heart badge, you'd know they were cool…," as she paused, I imagined the amount of stories that could have started with those little matt black hearts – "… and you'd probably be able to score, too."

She also prized things like the delicately embellished envelopes from Japanese fans, the elaborate lettering and drawings contrasting with the simple messages within, "I want to meet you Mr Sid Pistol".

There'd be a regular batch of more routine fan mail forwarded on from Virgin most days. We'd spend an afternoon dealing with the post and writing replies – usually adding a badge or two – as Sid was adamant that everyone should get a response. Other times though it would be a more familiar mixture of dope and daytime TV.

One hot afternoon we'd opened the windows to let some air in, only to be assaulted by the high-pitched whine from the paint sprayer in the repair shop beneath the flat. Eventually Nancy couldn't stand it any longer, exploding, "Jeez, they shouldn't be allowed to do that. Now I've got a fucking migraine!"

We went to the other room, but the noise and vibration were just as bad. Nancy's protests were getting louder. My reply that at least it would only be till the place closed at five wasn't what she wanted to hear

"Fuck sake Denis! Can't you go down there and tell them the woman upstairs is really ill with a migraine, and can they just turn that fucking thing off?"

As I trudged downstairs I knew it was a delusional moment, but felt that I had little choice but to go along with this fool's errand. I felt painfully aware of how stupid I looked, standing there in my Pistols t-shirt and leather jacket, asking the paint shop geezers if they'd mind not earning a living for an hour or two so Nancy could have some peace. Amazingly the sound had stopped by the time

I got back upstairs – presumably they were having a tea break. No sooner had Nancy started to thank me than the horrible metallic whine started up once more.

When Sid was around he was generally morose and irritable. As well as his drug intake, there were usually beers in the fridge now, and I soon learnt to be on my guard if he was drinking. Where he could take lethal doses of opiates without batting an eyelid, just one bottle of Pils was enough to halve his IQ and turn him into the archetypal leery and argumentative drunk. In addition, he'd started to develop a fixation with knives which I wasn't comfortable with. He'd often come back from his business trips uptown with a new one that he'd bought in Soho, and proudly show it off to Nancy and I, laughing as he'd flick the blade to and fro, making passes at an imaginary enemy.

One night Sid had been plucking idly at his bass as the TV played in the background – it must've been *Top of the Pops* – suddenly Nancy sprang forward to turn up the volume. She was always keen to check out any punk bands who came on, whether as old mates or potential competition but this time it was the promotional film for the Stones' 'Miss You' single. Sid stopped playing, and leant forward to squint at the screen. Soon they were both de-constructing the video in terms of how it showed the Stones trying to absorb punk influences, in terms of the sleazy back alley, dustbins and graffiti setting, the dramatic dark and doomy shadows, their hair a bit shorter and spikier and leather bomber jackets replacing the group's usual satin, velvet and crocodile-skin finery. Gaunt cheek bones featured prominently too. As always Sid was ready with a stream of sharp put downs, mainly scorning Jagger for "going disco" – but as with Presley, there was clearly a grudging respect just beneath the surface. Nancy was more interested from a music business perspective, going through the industry's various responses to punk, from trying initially to stamp it out or ignore it in the hope it'd go away. When that didn't work it had tried to smooth the sounds a little to be marketed as "New Wave" and now even established megastars like the Stones were realising that it'd be a good move to acknowledge some of the new style, if not the music.

We carried on talking about music and everything was fine until I asked Sid if he'd written any new songs, thinking that a solo album would be the next step once they'd got settled in New York. I was surprised at how angrily he reacted, banging his bass down, and asking me what the fuck I knew about songwriting. There wasn't much sign of the sharp and witty guy I'd known at Eton Avenue. Back then he'd always been adamant that, above anything else, he was going to stay the same and not get corrupted and changed by stardom and money. That kind of idealism was rarely in evidence either. At times I'd consider the irony of him now starting to act the big star and believe his own publicity – which really wasn't so surprising given how young he was and how fast everything had happened. He'd also acquired proper paid-up rock star mates like Lemmy and Phil Lynott and a taste for places more exclusive than The Marquee or The 100 Club. For all the brashness there were still times when he'd seem vulnerable and introspective, wondering if being blown around like a leaf in a storm was quite what he'd wanted when it all started. At such times I'd often think of the Peggy Lee classic, 'Is That All There Is?' – the offhand cynicism of the lyrics so skilfully hid the real fear underneath, and seemed to fit Sid's predicament so perfectly. Now, that would have been a stunning follow-up to 'My Way'…

Superficially the relationship between him and Nancy was less volatile, given their increased financial, domestic and narcotic security. They still did all the clingy and rather smothering mutual adoration and emotional dependency that I'd seen at my place, but there were dangerous areas just below the surface and were liable to erupt without warning.

At times Nancy seemed to adore him unconditionally as before, but at others there was a detached, almost aloof, feeling where she'd treat him like an incapable child who couldn't function without her to run his life. Now her role was managerial as well as romantic, these problems became more frequent. It was hard for him, too. He'd lost a lot of friends over his loyalty to Nancy, and it was, after all, his money that bankrolled everything they had.

Other unresolved and more personal tensions had carried over from Eton Avenue. One afternoon we sat around in their bedroom, uncomfortable in the oppressive heat. The windows stayed shut tight to keep out the noise from the garage. Nancy had stripped down to her underwear and was saying she wanted to go out shopping. Sid wasn't interested and ignored her. I could see the old danger signs. For a while a sultry sweaty silence took over, until he said, "Oi Nance, get us a drink. There's some cokes in the fridge".

Nancy concentrated on lighting her cigarette, pointedly ignoring him, before turning her attention to checking her fingernails. Sid tried again, before she snapped back, "I heard ya. You want a drink? Fucking get it yourself – you crippled or something?"

The hot torpor of the afternoon added to the tension in the air, but the argument seemed to have faded away until Sid suddenly turned, grabbing something off his bedside table, and in one movement swung back and uncoiled as he hit her hard across the top of the head, sending her cigarette flying. I looked up and saw a bunch of keys in his hand. I knew instinctively that it was wrong and I should say something, but then I'd most likely be out on the street within minutes. So cowardice, self-interest and short-term needs won out. It's like all the times I'd pull some stroke to get my drugs, half an hour's pleasure followed by thirty years of guilt – just as that afternoon's haunted me ever since.

I watched a trickle of dark red blood start to make its way down from Nancy's yellow-white hair, tracing the lines of her face, before meandering downwards, pausing briefly to mingle with her sweat in the hollow at the base of her neck, finally collecting in the cup of her bra. I wondered if she was about to retaliate, but she seemed more intent on not showing any reaction. After a few moments, she quietly said "You bastard!", before grabbing her gown and leaving the room.

I started to say something, but Sid simply said, "Don't!"

After the bedroom fight I knew it was time to move on. The dynamics had changed since the year before at my place and after such a hellish summer I was in desperate need of peace, stability and reflection. With nothing to my name but a raging habit I had no idea how to proceed, though. I felt too scrambled emotionally and chemically to face trying to sort things out with Annie, but knew that things were probably terminal this time, years of closeness erased in a moment's anger. Besides, the old squat zone was likely to be a dangerous place, prowled by predatory dealers and creditors.

One afternoon I asked Nancy if it'd be alright to crash there another night or two until I'd picked up my next Giro, and then be on my way. She looked up, and to my surprise she seemed disappointed, "You don't have to. Anyway, where ya gonna go? Not back to Annie, right? You should stay here, though I don't know how long till we go. Maybe you can take the place over later?"

As I thought it over, she suddenly became more animated, dashing to the hall and calling out, "Hey, I got an idea. Look, come on…"

I followed her out into the hall and watched as she yanked open a door. I'd always assumed it was some kind of walk-in cupboard, and even once the door was open, total darkness prevented me seeing any further.

"Fuck sake man, who took the fucking light bulb?" she

snarled.

Twenty minutes later I was back from the corner shop, standing on a rickety chair with Nancy holding it semi-steady as I changed the bulb. The perfect punk rock DIY couple. The light's glow struggled to illuminate the space around us. Now I could see we were in a small windowless room; walls, ceiling and floor painted black. A double mattress was propped against one wall, while some of Sid's guitars collected dust in a corner.

"So whaddya reckon? Not much of a view, sure, but you can stay here if you want."

Thinking of his near permanent scowl since the bedroom episode, I said, "Are you sure Sid's going to be okay with that?"

"Yeah yeah," she answered quickly, "don't worry, I'll fix Sid," giving me a mischievous little smile as she did so.

He was out on McLaren or Virgin Records post-Pistols duty most afternoons. Nancy chafed at her exclusion from these trips, both on a personal level and as a negation of her proclaimed "managerial" role – even though her authority didn't seem to extend beyond the confines of the flat as yet. They would go on shopping trips together, usually involving Soho, conveniently close to McLaren's PA, Sophie, who held the keys to the petty cash box. Sometimes they'd go to the methadone doctor in Chelsea – but when it came to the real business, she'd find herself home alone.

The next day I was making some tea in the kitchen when I heard the familiar chug of a taxi pulling up outside, followed by the street door opening and closing. I was expecting them both, but Nancy came in on her own, face almost hidden by a couple of huge and extravagant shopping bags. I realised that Sid had been detained elsewhere with business that didn't concern her, not that I said anything of course. We chatted as we drank our tea, but she was in a tetchy mood and I soon made a diplomatic retreat to the black box-room. I was reading the *NME* when she pushed the door open a while later, "You doing anything right now? Wanna see what I bought today?"

It was an order rather than a question. Suddenly her black top and leggings were on the floor and she was standing there in a shiny black leather basque, adorned with various straps and buckles which creaked and tinkled gently as she moved like the figurehead on some proud punk pirate ship. Before I could react, she continued, doing a twirl as she spoke, "It was one of those kinda fetish shops in Old Compton Street, round the corner from Glitterbest. Cost £160, right? Sid'll go nuts, but what was I supposed to do? Ya know – it's like 'Oh you're not wanted here now, you can piss off', and he doesn't say anything…" By now she'd lit a cigarette and sat on the bed beside me, barely contained by her new garment. "So whaddya think?"

I tried to think of a suitably neutral comment, like "It really suits you" or "I'm sure Sid'll like it", when she leant across me to stub her fag out. Leaning back, she smiled, reined in an errant breast, and said "You remember that time at your flat when Annie was over Highgate or some place?" I nodded, but before I could reply, she was on me, gently but firmly pushing me back, until she undid the top of my jeans with one hand and pulled the zip down with the other.

If the previous time – when she'd cut my hair – had been a natural, spontaneous and honest thing about two friends making love and recognising a growing affection between us, this time it was different: just sex, pure and simple, few words and no emotions. Nancy noticed that I wasn't exactly bursting with enthusiasm and decided to take charge of the situation. She started acting out a role-play where she was a hooker and I was her "john", as she put it, delivering a running commentary as she did so, "Now, this is what ya'd get if you were just an ordinary punter … but you always got some johns who are cool or pay a bit more – this is what I'd do for them or if I liked you…"

I wasn't complaining or resisting, but didn't feel totally cool with it either. It felt like she'd just ticked a few boxes on a checklist before moving on. After a while she'd got what she wanted or tired of the game and it was over as quickly and wordlessly as it had started, like a passing summer storm cloud.

Later we were sitting in the front room. I'd assumed that the same tacit agreement as before applied. Sid returned from his meeting sweaty and irritable, and sat on the sofa with a cold beer. Nancy bustled round, tidying up a bit, and chatting away all the while to no-one in particular, until she said in her most matter-of-fact voice, "So me and Denis decided we'd have a nice little fuck, you know, just to pass the time? Oh yeah, I shoulda said, I'd bought this leather basque – I'll show you later if you want".

A tremor passed through me. I tried not to show any reaction, but I hadn't expected her to be so casual and upfront. Sid's moods had become unpredictable of late, and I braced myself for whatever might come next.

"You can fuck who you want babe, you know that. It doesn't bother me," he replied, unfazed, and gave a quick nod in my direction. I wasn't entirely convinced by his casual reaction, but no more was said after that.

I'd noticed that Sid was scoring most days and generally flush with cash. I waited in the hope that he'd remember their last visit to Eton Avenue, when he'd ended up taking about £200 worth of the White Thai gear on credit as well as what they'd paid for. I'd already written off their unpaid share of the morphine tabs as history. I waited until Nancy was in a relaxed mood a day or so later. I knew I could be stepping on to thin ice, but tried to sound as casual as I could while pointing out that I really needed that money now. To be honest, I was annoyed at having to ask, and was starting to notice the disparity between all the talk of sticking by your mates and what actually went down. I tried to rationalise that he had a lot else on his mind as I waited for Nancy's reaction.

She seemed taken by surprise, and took her time before answering, "Uh, Sid's really kinda touchy about anything to do with money, you know? After all the shit going on with the Pistols and McLaren about money, he gets paranoid and thinks that's the only reason a lotta people want to know him now. It's best if I talk to him, okay?"

I hadn't really expected much more. He'd really bought into the Thunders attitude – if someone was dumb enough to hand over drugs without getting paid there and then, more fool them. I thought back over Sid's regular moans about being ripped off or overcharged for drugs and resigned myself to losing out. I also thought back to the old dealer's axiom when it came to whether to give credit or not – "No-One Likes Paying For Drugs They've Already Taken". So I was quite surprised when Nancy said she'd spoken to Sid and reminded him that I'd been good to them. He'd said I could have some of the stack of Virgin freebie albums that sat in the corner as their emergency cash reserve. I flicked through the pile. The early signs weren't good – about twenty copies of *Fish Rising* by Steve Hillage, some Mike Oldfield inevitably, but after that there were some tasty albums from the Front Line reggae series, along with some gems by The Ruts, and a few current chart hits like The Motors. Eventually I sorted out a viable selection and set off for the second-hand record shops in Camden.

It was a hot morning tramping round, but the load got ever lighter. It was still nowhere near the full amount Sid owed but at least I'd got some cash in my pocket again. Later that afternoon I headed back to Pindock Mews, stopping to buy a cold drink at the corner shop on the way. Opening the door, I was almost knocked over by Nancy charging down the narrow stairs. I immediately picked up on her anxiety and sensed danger in the air. After a second she panted breathlessly, "Sid's in a really crazy mood. You better be careful".

We went up to the front room. There was an aroma of recently smoked weed, but I could tell that Sid had started early on the beers from his red face and the empty Pils bottles scattered around the room. He held a half-drunk bottle in one hand, while he toyed with his new lock-knife in the other. To my surprise he asked if I wanted a beer, indicating a carrier bag on the floor. I shook my head and showed him my Coke can. Suddenly he was up on his feet, face contorted and close to mine as he shouted, "Why not? You've already helped yourself to my stuff, and that ain't the fucking half of it. Come on, nick something else – try your fucking luck and see what happens!"

The sinister little blade clicked open and he made a couple of passes in front of my face.

Nancy forced herself between us and pushed Sid back to the settee, trying to calm him down as she did so, "Hey, remember – you said he could have those albums…" I tried to join in, but she shook her head at me when I tried to speak, mouthing "Go" as she kept Sid at arm's length.

It was a horrible moment. I could see that he was beyond reason and prayed he'd calm down or pass out before taking it out on Nancy again. I hurried out into the incongruously beautiful sunshine, past the little garage downstairs and the fluttering floral baskets along the wall. I walked blindly around the streets, the most alone I'd ever been. I only stopped when the pavement ran out and the looming Westway took over, feeling the dust stick to me as I breathed in the car fumes and the smell of melting tar. The landmark of the motorway had mapped the early days of our friendship, but instinct told me that there would be no going back now.

That was the last time I saw them in person. I rang a couple of times when I thought Nancy might be there on her own, but she was slurred and out-of-it when we spoke. She grumbled that they should have been in New York weeks ago, but as usual they were holding on for money from McLaren. In any case, it sounded like it was full house too, whether Sid was there or not. It wasn't long till they were due to set off for New York. There were a couple of pretty ramshackle gigs at the Music Machine in Camden, last minute dashes for cash, with Nancy singing onstage at times, while a pale and puffy-faced Sid wandered about, beer bottle in hand. One of the sound crew tagged along to an after show session at the Mews, flew too high and was found dead the next morning on the white leather settee where I'd sat and crashed so recently. The shadows were starting to grow darker and close in.

THE END

POSTSCRIPT

Chelsea Hotel

I've tried as much as possible to restrict myself to things that I was actually involved in or witnessed – which is why there's so little about the fateful US tour, for example – but it'd be too much of a cop-out not to talk about the sad events that scarred the winter of '78/79. There's speculation to this day about what happened, and people have virtually made careers from mining every possible angle of Sid and Nancy's deaths, with the Chelsea Hotel and its long Bohemian history providing as much opportune padding as required. Given the cast of resident and transient addicts, desperadoes, mysterious passing strangers and others eager to reveal their unique insights – many years later, generally – it's easy to generate a snowstorm of conflicting possibilities and culprits.

But there was a scene I'd witnessed, and been part of, so many times. The desperate drug hunt – but this time with no shortage of ready cash – all dressed up and nowhere to go. I knew how they would take a perverse pleasure when they were strung out in taunting and goading each other. There was a momentum to these scenes – almost like a set script or ritual – which often culminated in a scuffle after the words had stopped working. This time, though, the gods played a wild card and it all went irreversibly wrong.

All that damp dismal autumn I scoured the papers and music magazines for every possible detail, hoping that through reading I'd somehow penetrate the truth beneath the mounting heaps of distortion and mischief. With the tabloid press revelling in the demise of their top hate figure of the day, drooling over a story that would likely run for months with lots of extra sales, there was no shortage of people with sensational "inside" stories to tell and sell. I bought papers like *New York Rocker* and the *Village Voice* along with the usual American music mags in the hope of getting a more local, "ground up" perspective. All the extra voices only added to the confusion. Occasionally instinct kicked in. I read the story related by one of the Chelsea lowlifes about how Sid had come to him that night depressed and disillusioned, and given him the leather jacket with white reveres seen in so many photos (a gift from Heartbreakers' drummer Jerry Nolan) along with all their scrapbooks and mementoes. Alarm bells went off instantly in my head. I knew that jacket was possibly Sid's favourite garment, and there was no way he'd have presented it to someone he barely knew. I could imagine the process of rumours and whispers, before the scavengers emerged and headed for Sid and Nancy's room in search of any rich pickings in the chaotic debris of their room. Lying, thieving bastard, I thought. He wasn't the only one.

When something mysterious, chaotic or confusing happens, it's easy to get lost in Patti Smith's "sea of possibilities" to the point where nothing's certain and everything you thought you knew is cancelled out by something else. Once upon a time there was a theory known as "Occam's Razor". This proposes that if you're trying to solve a problem and there are competing solutions or theories, the one that requires the least amount of prior assumptions is most likely to be right. If I look out of the window and see a light in the sky, it's more likely to be a plane, meteor or firework than a passing UFO or vision of the Virgin Mary.

As soon as I heard that Nancy was dead, I had a very clear thought amid the shock and sadness. I knew that it was Sid. I didn't want to believe it, but it was a gut feeling, and one I've never doubted since. I don't think that he meant to, and in a really grim twist I don't think he even knew for sure if he'd done it or not.

The initial reports were confusing, just mentioning that drugs were involved. I knew that Nancy was too experienced a user to have OD'd, as she was always complaining how weak New York heroin was compared to London's supply. Once I knew she'd been stabbed there was only one explanation. Given what I understand of the circumstances of that night – Sid desperately trying to block out withdrawal with heavy downers like Tuinal while Nancy tried to sort out a genuine deal from all the rip-off artists wanting to disappear into the night with cash up front. Take enough downers like that and they'll erase your short-term memory, just like an alcohol blackout. It's the same process: coming round heavily hung over and near brain dead, then trying to reconstruct the night through tracing your body map of bumps, burns and bruises until someone tells you just what a prat you were the night before.

I'd seen so much violence between them, at my place and at Pindock Mews, that there was really no mystery or surprise in what had happened. Even so, it didn't lessen the impact of her dying. Death wasn't new to me, but this was the first time someone younger than me had died. I don't recall crying, simply feeling numb, oblivious to my mother reminding me that's what happens when you get in with the wrong crowd, and asking what had happened to all my nice friends. In the upheaval of my abrupt departure from Pindock Mews and the escalation of events in New York, I'd forgotten a simple fact like how close she and I had been at times.

If violence becomes an inbuilt part of a relationship – with the added complications of addiction and desperation – it will only be a matter of time before things get out of control. I thought back to the horrible scene in their bedroom at their place, and some of the things that went

down at Eton Avenue when Annie and I had sheltered in
our little cave and Misha dived under their bed as blows
were traded and the air teemed with threats and abuse. It
only needed to be stepped up a degree or two more to get
really serious. Sid's fixation with knives took them past the
"good old days" of just fists, belts and buckles and soon
he was to reach the point of no return. Although I didn't
see it at the time, there's a very revealing clip (easily found
online) of Sid and Nancy on a cable TV show with Stiv
Bators and Cynthia Ross. Most of the show is knockabout
fun and everyone seems pretty out of it. When they get to
the phone-in things get even more raucous, with Nancy
adopting her strange "Mockney" accent while threatening
a potential Sid groupie. Sid seems particularly affected by
whatever he's on – Coke? Alcohol? Speed?– and is rude
and aggressive with callers, just yelling out crude abuse at
all and sundry, to sycophantic laughter all round. It's a long
way from the subtle, observational humour, or the kind
of ironic self-mocking wordplay I knew from before. It's
an uncomfortable piece of viewing for me, like watching
someone teetering on a tightrope while the crowd go crazy
below.

     In no time at all John Peel was playing a heavy dub
reggae track called 'Pistol Boy' by a New York MC known as
Militant Barry – "Mi really wanna know who guilty a' deh
killing". It's a great cut, hard to find now, but well worth the
effort of tracking down. I took momentary comfort from
Mr Barry's view that Sid had been set up by the authorities
for being too out front in disrespecting Babylon system and
inciting the youth with his bad example – but I knew it
wasn't true.

     With the constant press coverage, it was no surprise
that it all started to spill over into my dreams. The tabloids
gloated gleefully over an allegedly tearful Sid begging to
be spared Christmas in jail (he got bail, fortunately), and I
remembered how surprisingly sentimental he and Nancy

had been about that time of year. The other big media event of the day was *Star Wars* and soon my mind conflated the two stories. One night I dreamt I was visiting Sid at the notorious Riker's Island prison. We were in a large open plan room, dimly lit by flickering neon lights and all the furniture bolted down to the floor. Not unlike the local dole office apart from the black-uniformed guards with Darth Vader helmets sitting in each corner. Suddenly I was sitting there, with Sid on the other side of a reinforced glass window.

The strange internal logic of dreams has always fascinated me. Sometimes they present the complete opposite of reality, but they can also give a perspective on life that's subtly different but also more true in a way. I knew I should be angry at him – after all we'd parted on bad terms, and I'd cared about Nancy a lot. His distress was intense and almost tangible. He promised me that he'd never meant to kill her, and this time I believed him. He seemed to have been reduced to a little lost child who just wanted to go home, but knew it was too late now for forgiveness or another chance. Then the mists closed in and he was gone. I awoke with an unsettled feeling – the dream had been so intense and physically real – but also knowing that my feelings towards him had been resolved.

Sid and Nancy have continued to put in very occasional surreal appearances. Sometimes we've been back at Eton Avenue, frantically searching for some lost dope, or listening to Sid bantering away at the TV. The last time it was just Nancy. She was on some kind of celebrity TV show. She looked older and more sophisticated, with her hair still blonde but tied back and sporting a sassy chic red beret. Then I realised I was actually in the studio with her. I could tell she wasn't addicted any more, but as I started to speak, the dream faded away…

There was nothing dream-like about Sid's death in February '79. Nancy's death had been shocking and unexpected, but there was a grim inevitability this time. The same media process kicked into gear, soon generating a mass of conflicting theories, just as with Nancy. All this tended to obliterate the poignancy of another young person dead way before his time. It's continued to the present day… There's the suicide theory, brought on either by him being unable to cope without Nancy, or knowing that he faced years buried in an American jail. In an added refinement, it's alleged that his mother was the agent and instigator of his exit. Another version has it that Sid was the victim of a "hot shot" – a planned hit where he was deliberately given pure (or poisoned) heroin.

Given his situation at the time, the suicide argument is certainly plausible, but once again I'd get out the razor, cut through the distractions and suggest the simplest solution is the most likely one. Sid had a gargantuan appetite for drugs and always wanted to get his drugs inside him as quickly as he could. He'd be disappointed if he wasn't left reeling by the rush. I know from my own experiences how there are few things an addict fears more (apart from No Dope) than a weak fix that doesn't do anything. It's so easy to think that even with reduced tolerance, it'd be best to put in a little bit more, just to make sure… Sid would usually take the whole lot at once, regardless of the amount. So for me there was no mystery or conspiracy, just the sad waste of another young life.

A mere three weeks later, Sid's version of the Eddie Cochran classic 'C'mon Everybody' was rushed out, followed in the summer by 'Something Else'. Typically the business hedged its bets, both singles sporting Vicious-themed cover art but maintaining the Sex Pistols' brand identity. It was strange suddenly seeing the video of Sid tearing through sunlit English countryside on a motorbike, at last living out his dream. The songs had been recorded the same time as 'My Way' but Sid had never mentioned them to me. Being wise after the event, one can't help finding something unsettling and prescient in the choice of cover material – both men died aged twenty-one. Of course it's easy enough to see it simply as yet another case of the music industry cashing in on a performer's death, but I couldn't help feeling a simple pleasure that in the end, Sid had "shown them all" as he'd promised – even if it had cost him his life along the way.

Years went by, and punk became just another memory for me, and another marketing label for the mainstream nostalgia industry. I generally kept quiet about my association with Sid and Nancy for a variety of reasons – I hate name-dropping, I was doing everything I could to free myself from the heroin era and I wasn't sure people would even believe me. I didn't pay any attention to Alex Cox's *Sid and Nancy* film in 1986 until a friend told me that his normally disaffected and cynical teenage son had been reduced to tears watching it, and had become obsessed with punk thereafter.

I'd expected Sid – let alone Nancy – to be gradually shunted off into footnote status as the Official History of Punk preferred to concentrate on Pistols' reunion tours or the big names like Johnny Rotten and Joe Strummer. Meanwhile the Thatcher dictatorship ground on in its mean-minded, money obsessed way while the musical mainstream seemed to get more blatantly cynical and exploitative. More and more though I started to notice kids wearing Sid Vicious t-shirts instead of the ubiquitous Nirvana or smiley face designs. Sid and Nancy were coming back and this time they would be here to stay.

One of the most surprising things for me when I first started writing this was to find the huge amount of general punk material online, a lot of which was dedicated to Sid and/or Nancy. I'd asked a couple of Sid t-shirt wearers what the attraction was. The response would always be along the lines that at least he was "real" compared to the music icons of their day, where rebellion was just another stage on the corporate career path for most bands. That, or on a basic level, that Sid "didn't give a fuck". Meanwhile Nancy had become the poster girl and soul mate of unhappy and disaffected teenagers and young women all over the planet, though the original hate lobby have their descendants as well.

While writing this I've had some fascinating talks and communications with people who were involved in the scene and have made it through intact. There's been just as much interaction with new generations of punks, fans, musicians, misfits and artists.

Heroin Reflections

There are times when I'd rather write about anything else but heroin addiction. Unfortunately it is as much part of this story as any of the characters or the punk scene itself. There aren't any easy answers when considering addiction. Even the simplest question – why should otherwise intelligent young people not only submit themselves to all the problems that come with addiction, but fiercely defend their right to do so? It does seem strange from my viewpoint now – off heroin for nearly thirty years – that we clung so loyally to our chains, and still trot out the bogus argument of the artist as sensitive soul who needs serious drugs as a source both of inspiration and insulation from the uncaring dullard society around us.

Even now I'm not sure of the answers. I might have got over the worst of the cravings, but there's rarely a day when something doesn't make me think of heroin, and I still know how easily it can creep up and take you unawares. I can remember the initial attraction of the drug, but to give up twelve years of my life to that endless pursuit? I'd experienced most of the heroin spectrum in the first couple of years, after that it was simply repetition, which of course is the whole point of addiction. Equally, I'm not comfortable with the usual evasions like "That wasn't me – it was just the effect of the drugs – I'm different now". It was me. It still is. I still inhabit the same body. It was my choice.

There's probably an element of exorcism here, too, hoping that if I dive deep enough I can banish some of the lurking shadows in my mind. An old friend who knew me then now accuses me of still being obsessed by heroin, even though it is long ago in the past now. For her, I'm still getting vicarious thrills by wallowing in drug-porn to the extent that there's a part of me that's always addicted. Apparently I make it all sound so cool and attractive that she won't let her grown-up son read this book lest he get tempted.

My own introduction to the drug came during the winter of '73. I'd come back from a great summer in New York to a dismal autumn. I went back to the shared house in a little village outside Cambridge, but soon felt bored and restless. I tried to suppress the nagging realisation that I'd made a mistake coming back here to nothing in particular when there'd been so many possibilities in New York. I'd had many good times there with my friends, but now it just felt like repetition and it was time to move on.

As usual we'd made a weekend trip over to Paul and Jan's, friends who lived in another village close by. We had quite a lot in common – aside from the Grateful Dead and cricket, we were both on the lookout for drugs other than cannabis and trips. We'd had a few ultimately unsatisfactory weekends shoving heavily-cut coke up our noses to little effect. They'd converted the garage at their place into a kind of clubhouse with the mandatory early 70's mix of wall-hangings, posters, bean bags and floor cushions. I settled down for "Another Saturday Night".

Halfway through the evening Paul quietly informed me that he'd scored some heroin, and would I be interested in taking some with him and Jan? While I considered the offer, he asked if anyone else wanted some. They each looked up from their joint-rolling and replied in turn, "No, I'm fine thanks Paul". At last it was my turn to decide. With a head full of Burroughs, Trocchi, Anna Kavan and other opium promoters, and wallowing in Stones' drug adverts like 'Sister Morphine' and 'Dead Flowers', my choice was inevitable. I was the only one to volunteer. I'm not sure now what was so attractive about the imagery of "I'll be in my basement room/With a needle and a spoon…" – which precisely foretold Eton Avenue – but I knew I wanted to go that bit further, and, in any case I knew all about the dangers of addiction from my reading, and that wasn't going to happen to me, was it?

Paul and Jan were old hands when it came to hard drugs. We went upstairs to their bedroom, where Paul quickly and efficiently sorted out their gear and got ready to inject. Before doing so he put out what looked like a couple of absurdly small, barely visible lines. Oh well, that'll be another experience to tick off, I thought, as I snorted it up. Almost immediately I felt a gagging reaction in my throat and thought I was going to throw up. All very different to the cold, numb chemical coke backdrop I was used to. The momentary nausea passed. I noticed Paul getting another fix together and decided to head back downstairs.

By then I could feel the new drug spreading through my system. The queasy feeling was still there, but seemed irrelevant compared to the warmth spreading through my body and the intensifying high that was beginning to fill my head. The warm bubble inside took shape and got stronger. I felt acutely aware of how my blood pulsed as it circulated round me, buzzing in my ears as it did so. It was a different feeling to knock-out strength hash, though. Along with the sensation of spacey detachment, there was a surge of energy as well. I felt my skin and flesh become synthetic, like some kind of rubbery plastic, while the veins and nerves turned into wires and cables transporting the new sensation to every corner of my system.

Meanwhile the others had reached the mellow stage of the evening, as indicated by the country rock soundtrack. I'd never paid much attention to the lyrics of the Dead's *American Beauty* album much before, but now they seemed to open out like the pages of a book. I realised though that I seemed to miss out on entire tracks, and wasn't sure why. I noticed a couple of slightly anxious looks cast in my direction. Suddenly it seemed too much of an effort to concentrate on the music. My eyelids felt heavy, hooded and vulture-like. I realised I was desperate for a cigarette, lit up a Camel and lay back amongst the floor cushions.

The need to close my eyes was impossible to resist. I let the mix of music, background chatter and tobacco smoke waft and swirl about me and through my head. I didn't yet understand the intensity of the dream – or its intense reality – but next I realised I'd time-slipped back a few months to the summer. Riding Greyhound buses and hitching rides through the South in a vain attempt to get to New Orleans via William Faulkner and the blues. There'd been a truck-stop somewhere in South Carolina, and now I was there again – keeping my head down, literally, staring intently at the laminated table top. There was an intense, cinematic quality to the hyper-real colours and at times it all felt too beguiling to leave behind before I knew what would happen next but I wanted to tell the others about how great this was too. I'd open my eyes and sit up, but maybe just another minute…

I realised my friend Bun was talking to me. I forced my eyes open, and accepted the joint she was offering me. I jerked out of my virgin nod (see also "gouch", "mong" and "kissing the carpet" in the standard dictionary of dope slang). I noticed that the longed-for cigarette had burnt out in the ashtray, barely touched. I took a drag on the joint, enjoying the tactile sensation of the smoke, drawing it in and exhaling slowly. As far as effect was concerned though, the hash seemed to barely register compared to the more powerful process in my head. This felt very different to the communal get-stoned-together cannabis scene or the intense near-telepathy of acid trips. By contrast, this felt more like a personal initiation in to some secret knowledge and had a private quality to it. Then the analytical thoughts became too demanding, and suddenly the truck stop was calling me back. This time it was dawn and I was sitting outside, looking at the crumpled paper cups blowing around the yard. I must stay awake or I'll miss my Greyhound connection, but there's this bit of paper, blowing around my feet. It could be my ticket, so I lean forward to pick it up…

Just as I was about to grasp it, I felt a light touch on my arm. Opening my eyes, I saw Bun leaning over me, looking concerned, "Sorry to wake you Denis – are you feeling alright? You looked like you were going to drop that joint". I was just about to tell her how many light-years beyond simply "alright" I felt when another feeling kicked in. I swallowed hard and felt moisture in my mouth. I was going to be sick.

Right now.

I dragged myself upright and pushed past a surprised Bun, making it to the bathroom just in time. Normally I hated being sick, but this was more like blowing my nose or clearing my throat, leaving me cleansed for more action, and all a long way from the grim mess of a night-ending drunken chunder.

Paul and Jan had come down from upstairs with a couple more lines for me. The night continued in a cycle of nodding, drifting and dreaming, the occasional bathroom run, and rapping with my new drug buddies. We sat apart in our exclusive little group on one side of the room, while the others sat in a huddle, as if by a camp fire, still rolling their joints.

It all looked very hard work. They were surrounded by overflowing ashtrays and empty fag packets. It was a constant task to maintain their high and keep the balloon aloft. Whereas I had merely inhaled a couple of times and was cruising the heavens with Thomas de Quincey and Bill Burroughs.

By now it was late into the night. Even though it was a new experience, I could tell I'd be riding this high till the morning. I also had the feeling that this was a significant moment that went beyond the box-ticking of trying another new drug. For a while I'd been looking for a change from the ever-weaker cannabis, but the alternatives weren't that attractive, either. Cocaine was okay, but somehow never quite lived up to expectations (and what passed for coke then was usually a heavily diluted, fine white powder). I'd never liked speed or had much time for its enthusiasts. To me it was an idiot's drug for the easily pleased – staying up all night? Wow! Give that man a medal! I'd had enough of psychedelics, and didn't see the appeal of Mandrax (Quaaludes in the US), a non-surgical home lobotomy that combined most of the less attractive features of being drunk.

I've always been resistant to clichés about "love at first sight" in any context, but I knew that that first taste was going to lead to a lasting attraction. Heroin seemed to combine all my favourite drug scenes into one convenient package. Hash sessions would start out well but drag on past the point of interest, petering out into long, oppressive silences, broken only by the occasional attack of the munchies. By comparison this new experience was intense, compressed and darkly seductive.

It felt like a private bond between the three of us that night. At the time it felt noble, artistic and blood brotherly, our own little elite drug clique – unaware or uncaring of the isolation that lay ahead. The flat at Eton Avenue and serious injecting habits were four or five years in the future, away from those easy going rustic scenes.

This sad illusion of togetherness was something we'd all be clinging on to grimly in self-justification by the time Annie, Sid, Nancy and I came together at the flat. By then it was about isolation and survival, rather than gourmet highs, and facing up to the grim knowledge that we'd burnt our boats long ago and were committed to the long ride of addiction and wherever it might lead. Allow me though the innocent and inquisitive pleasure of that first night, as I drifted off, cosseted by the knowledge of the little foil wrap nestling in the pocket of my cheesecloth shirt.

A Warning from the Future

Word of the session at Paul's had got out, and soon another old mate, John the Sculptor, came round looking eager and expectant. I knew from talking to him before that he'd had previous with hard drugs back in the States, so it wasn't that much a surprise when he turned up looking for a turn-on. We were at a friend's place – in a strange foreshadowing of later events, Annie and Ella were there too – and as I didn't want to get my taboo drugs out in front of everyone, I passed him the packet discreetly, assuming he'd slip off for a sensible little line.

A few moments later we heard a crash from upstairs. I dashed up to find John lying on the bathroom floor turning blue. I picked up the packet from the floor – he'd injected almost all of it. One moment it had been a bunch of friends sitting round having a good time. Now death was breaking into our comfortable little scene and I was surrounded by a circle of accusing faces. I tried to excuse myself on the grounds of ignorance and innocence.

John came round a couple of minutes later, blinked a couple of times as he found his glasses, and looked up at me, beaming, "Hey man, that's some righteous shit! Have you got any more?"

Later that day I was back at my place. I looked at the little packet with revulsion, crumpled it up and tossed it in the bin. I wasn't planning on tempting fate again. It was my first experience of my new love's dark side, but I was too arrogant to take any notice. It'd be the first of many occasions when I'd reject advice or warnings with an abrupt, "Yeah, but I'm not going to do that", or some glib nonsense

about life just being a matter of discovering your addiction
of choice (if I was in a reasonably polite mood), but more
often I'd respond dismissively with a half-remembered
borrowing from one of the early William Burroughs books,
"The problem isn't addiction but supply".

Just as years later the arrival of Barry, the scheming
sneak thief, should have warned us that we were starting to
stray into dangerous territory, so that near fatal first warning
was as clear as could be. Of course the vast majority of
people never go anywhere near heroin, and of those who
do, only a very few progress to serious addiction, generally
deciding that hours of vomiting the next day outweighed
any fleeting pleasures. Nor do most people have the appetite
or inclination for the sheer repetition of having to do the
same things day after day as part of the iron timetable of
addiction but to the addict the constant repetition is a form
of narcotic brainwashing, a kind of normalisation process.

Somewhere along the line a mainstream publisher got
interested in my Sid and Nancy memoirs. I duly supplied a
synopsis and a couple of sample chapters as requested, and
eagerly awaited the next development. I passed the time
deciding how I'd spend the advance. Eventually word came
back: they loved what they'd read and thought it was really
original and unusual. There was one problem, though –
could I please take out some of the drug-taking as it wasn't
necessary to include it in every chapter? I replied that
writing about four addicts living together made that rather
difficult and in many ways the repetition was the whole
point. I heard no more from them after that.

Even later, when Sid, Nancy and Eton Avenue were
distant memories, a concerned but bewildered relative
asked why, as an intelligent and educated person, I'd kept
on doing something that had caused so much chaos and
stress for me and anyone who'd strayed into my orbit. She
listened intently as I explained that if I was doing something

I enjoyed, it'd be even better – and usually last longer – if I was suitably drugged. And better still, if I was feeling bored or pissed off, my mood would invariably be lifted by a little hit.

For once Auntie Rita was silenced. She shook her head slowly before looking me directly in the eye "Well, I can't see any hope for you in that case".

Some Facts and Figures

My heroin career lasted around twelve years, probably ten of which involved regular daily injecting. Taking a rough average of around four or five hits a day that would make around 1825 times a year. Looking at the overall timespan, the figure must be somewhere around 20,000 times. No wonder it was often so hard to find a vein.

It's harder to calculate money-wise. At the beginning in 1973/74 heroin cost £20 per gram. This rose through the decade, peaking at around £80 during some serious droughts, very occasionally dropping to £40, but generally settling at around £60 a gram. In many ways the market reflected similar processes to the cannabis market not only in price fluctuations but also in reduced market choice. Just as most hash was Moroccan by the end of the decade, the heroin market had been almost completely taken over by brown Persian gear. There were times of famine, of course, and times of plenty – during one of the Singapore episodes we were taking around three grams a day each. A carefully saved last ounce was meant to help us taper off gently – it lasted us little more than three days. So allowing for a daily average of half a gram at around £25 we're looking at a figure or around £175 a week in seventies money – around £9,000 a year in "old money", and something like £90,000 or more for the whole period. Multiply by five or so to get a figure approximate to today's rates of exchange.

So what is the point of this? The physical side of addiction is well known, but the psychological side is just as important and more long-lasting. One of the main themes in writing this has been to emphasise the sheer unrelenting pressure and repetition of addiction. There are elements of brainwashing in the effect of performing the same ritualised actions every day, thousands of times. When things go wrong for the addict, and that daily action list is "withdrawn", a trapdoor opens to an abyss of pain and panic. Or does it? In many ways withdrawal most closely resembles an extended panic attack – how do you fill all those gaps in the day? Think of the last time you were without your phone or other favourite device for a day. The "horrors of withdrawal" are in many ways the addict's trump card – how often did we justify ourselves with a plaintive "You don't know what it's like".

The physical side is unpleasant, of course – aching bones and tense muscles, alternating hot flushes and goose pimples, upset stomach, and so on – but after the first couple of times I knew what to expect and learnt to put up with it. What I found difficult was the feeling of zero energy, and an all-encompassing depressive "What's the point?" response to any thought beyond scoring. Some say that heroin withdrawal, like Room 101 in George Orwell's *1984* will find a way to adapt itself to each user's potential weaknesses. I've never been a good sleeper, and it would be the never-ending succession of sleepless nights that would wear me down to the point of desperation, when the simplest thought or act of communicating becomes a strain.

Many times when we didn't have any gear I'd see Sid and Nancy resort to injecting tap water, in the hope that performing the usual ritual – albeit missing the key ingredient – might bring some relief. Of course it didn't, often having the opposite effect of heightening their anxiety. For all the dread with which addicts whisper the dread word "withdrawal", greater life experience since then suggests that there's a big element of self-dramatising in the whole process. Physically the majority of symptoms are like an attack of 'flu. A bad attack, maybe – but one which can be relieved simply enough. It doesn't cause lasting damage. People don't suffer heart attacks or strokes as a result of "cold turkey", nor does it turn into blood-poisoning, pneumonia or anything else life-threatening. It's a matter of how one handles it. Nancy was scornful of anything she saw as weakness when we were sick, however Annie could never cope and would disintegrate into alternating tears and rages at the first ache or sniffle. Sometimes we'd try to bond and get through it together, at others we'd remember why Jean Paul Sartre once said "Hell is other people". I'd sneer her at her with remarks like, "Hey, hold the front page! Headline news – Annie hasn't had her drugs!"

It's all part of the reductive, brutalising effect of addiction, and the narrowing down of thoughts and feelings to a pragmatic and selfish world view. You're either stoned or you aren't. You're okay for tomorrow. The bottom line soon takes over. Slowly resentments get dwelt on and saved up for future recriminations. Then there are the landmarks along the way, each one making it harder to turn back, and making their own little "Addicts Checklist"…

- The first time you decide you'd rather get high by yourself than with other people.

- The first time strung out.

- The first time shooting up.

- The first time you convince yourself it'll be okay to spend the rent money scoring, and really believing you'll make it up later.

Then there are the more subtle indicators…

- Blowing out old, non-using friends for solo time getting high or hanging out with new drug buddies.

- Cancelling a prior engagement because you've got to score or are otherwise engaged in drug business.

- The first lie to cover up your addiction. Lying to other people, that is. You'll have been deceiving yourself for a long time already by then.

- Abandoning things you've enjoyed before in favour of getting stoned.

- Realising that one of your drug friends has ripped you off.

- Cheating on your "us against the world" drug partner is a big line to cross, the first time one of you thinks, "No, I'm not sharing this time".

I'm not religious, but sometimes I'd remember the powerful biblical imagery of the column of smoke by day and the column of fire at night and feel a connection. In the end, it would narrow down to a blazing path that keeps you locked in the present moment and whatever needs to be done. Abolish the past. Do what you have to. Take care of business. Don't worry about what a few minutes' impulsive behaviour does in terms of trashing your family and ruining friendships – until you realise that those are the things that matter more than a few moments in the drug zone. Heroin induces a real passivity – combine that with the kind of narrowed-down world I've tried to describe, and it's easy to drift into a placid and fatalistic acceptance.

Get straight for thirty minutes. Feel bad for thirty years.

And then there are the categories like "Dead Friends" and "OD's and other near-death experiences".

"Born to Lose", as Thunders would have put it…

Sid, Nancy and Heroin

There's always been a mixture of guesswork, speculation and fantasy around Sid and Nancy's heroin use. Given the tragic conclusion of their lives – particularly Sid's OD – it is inevitable that people wonder why and how the drug was such a defining element in their relationship, and who was the driving force in their ready acceptance of the addict lifestyle? Did Nancy – as has been alleged – use heroin and sex as a way of luring an unsuspecting and trusting Sid into supporting her long-term addiction? There was certainly an element of bonding in their joint drug use, a defiant celebration and affirmation of their bond. Equally, there's a view that Nancy and the Heartbreakers were solely responsible for introducing the heroin use that blighted the UK punk scene. This is a key issue for the "Nauseating Nancy" hate lobby. And of course, in this narrative, it is Sid's drug use that sows the seed for the demise of the Pistols.

Nancy was certainly no innocent where heroin was concerned. She never pretended to be. There was none of the overwrought hand-wringing of many addicts, just acceptance that she'd made her choice. Anyway, the whole process of getting clean was way too long and demanding, and after all, what would be the point, when she'd only be returning to the same screwed-up normality she'd been trying to escape in the first place? She'd tell us about her hardcore experiences in New York, supporting her habit as a sex worker or dancing in clubs. Generally her voice would drop down low and slow, sometimes faltering over a really painful memory, but sometimes she seemed to revel in getting deep down in all the degrading detail.

I thought back to the teeming streets and choking subways of New York, the sheer volume and intensity of all that humanity crammed together – London had seemed a sleepy village by comparison. Not a good place to be an addict, for sure, especially not a young woman. Sometimes living on the streets, her life had been a desperate round of hustling, and then trying to get a decent deal from the local gangsters without being raped. And so it went on. It wasn't all bad, though – she'd brighten up as she'd talk about her friendship with Debbie Harry who'd helped and guided her on the scene, as they worked the clubs together, Nancy gritting her teeth as a strung-out go-go dancer. One time Annie clutched my hand as we listened. I looked across and saw her eyes brimming with tears. She leant over to give her a sisterly hug of support and empathy, but Nancy shrugged it away. That's what life was like, did Annie think she couldn't take it?

Given that Nancy came to London in the wake of the notorious Heartbreakers, it's no surprise that the heroin label is so firmly attached to her. The group were bound to get media attention with their New York Dolls' connections, and the still fresh memories of their 1973 visit which had ended with the tragic drug-connected death of drummer Billy "Billy Dolls" Murcia. It wasn't long before hints were dropped in the music press that maybe the group ran on something other than the spirit of rock 'n' roll. In Johnny Thunders and Jerry Nolan they possessed two of the most hardcore "schmeckers" in any shooting gallery, as well as two stylish cats who just oozed New York street attitude. Apart from The Stranglers and The Vibrators, the English punk bands were young guys, if not always fresh-faced. The Heartbreakers had clearly been round the block a few times, and their whole demeanour – dress, hair, New York slang, cheek bones, all razor sharp – indicated that they were the real deal.

There are still those who persist in the belief that the UK punk scene was destroyed by the Heartbreakers' introduction of heroin to the other groups on the famous *Anarchy* tour, and this view is often extended as a justification or argument for hating Nancy (guilt by association?). Generally – but not always – this goes with the view that punk was something thought up by Malcolm McLaren sometime in the mid-70's (before those brash Americans came and gatecrashed the party). I've discussed this point with someone who was part of the tour, and was involved with the scene before it even had a name. He, too, succumbed to heroin addiction as the decade went on, but was adamant that the temptations were all local – and that if anything Johnny Thunders and the others were more intent on eeking out their supplies than in turning everybody else on. In any case, the group would have had to have been followed by an opiate supertanker to have sustained the burgeoning heroin scene of the late 70's and early 80's. I don't want to diminish the sadness of the deaths of Sid, Nancy, and all the others, but once again, there's a far more straightforward explanation in the tidal wave of Persian brown heroin dominating the scene then.

The Pistols' manager had previous with the Dolls, having overseen their bizarre red leather and Communist imagery late period before everything disintegrated in chaotic rancour. However farcically the episode had ended though, it had given him the opportunity to spot the punk scene developing in the city and take notes assiduously as well as giving him access to the Heartbreakers as they emerged from the valley of the Dolls. Mix and match with the perforce torn and pinned clothes sported by early Heartbreaker Richard Hell, stand back and see what happens. Thus the Heartbreakers were summoned to London to take part in the first *Anarchy* Tour, with Nancy arriving in their wake soon after.

There was another advantage in the group's relocation

to England. London had a far more varied range of much stronger dope than New York, and cheaper too. There seemed to be more and more Persian Brown by the day, White Thai, but most of all the legendary Chinese Rocks, a brand which took no prisoners. There have been disputes since then as to who contributed what to the song between Dee Dee Ramone and Johnny Thunders. It's a shame, but that shouldn't detract from the power and economy of the lyrics. There's never been any shortage of songs about hard drugs from the jazz era onwards, whether celebrating or condemning. Bert Jansch's 'Needle of Death' was probably the first one I heard, and of course there are well-known songs like 'The Needle and the Damage Done' or 'Golden Brown', but nothing sums things up as pithily as 'Chinese Rocks'. The lyrics are concise and ruthlessly to the point, dripping with inside knowledge and framed with the fatalistic black humour that often accompanies addiction:

> *Somebody called me on the phone*
> *They said hey, is Dee Dee home?*
> *Do you wanna take a walk?*
> *Do you wanna go cop?*
> *Do you wanna go get some Chinese Rocks?*

> *Chorus:*
> *I'm living on a Chinese Rock*
> *All my best things are in hock*
> *I'm living on Chinese Rocks*
> *Everything's in the pawn shop*

> *The plaster's falling off the wall*
> *My girlfriend's crying in the shower stall*
> *It's hot as a bitch, I shoulda been rich*
> *But I'm just diggin' this Chinese ditch"*

(Repeat chorus twice)

Is this glamourizing hard drug use? You decide…

Since the first eruption of punk in summer '76, it had been interesting to see how the scene became more audible and visible, gradually easing aside the pub rock bands of the last few years, or simply fly-posting over the big mainstream gigs at Earl's Court and Hammersmith. Among the many little tremors and undercurrents were some stark Track Records posters, white lettering on a black background – "The Heartbreakers – Chinese Rocks" – appearing around Camden and the rest of town. These were followed by Chinese Rocks t-shirts, black with the same Fu Manchu type lettering, and avidly sought after by those in the know.

I had a passing encounter with the group and their entourage when trying to recover a drug debt, finding them much amused at the naïvety of someone who'd handed out hard drugs on credit and finding the whole London trip a bit of an adventure. Back home in New York – in those pre-AIDS days – there had been no legitimate source of syringes, which had to be stolen, improvised or otherwise sourced. One of Nancy's favourite stories of the group's pioneer days in London was of the time they were told of chemists like Hall's in Piccadilly which sold everything an addict needed. This sounded like such an obvious put-on – like striped paint – that none of the group would go on such a fool's errand. After all, they weren't some bunch of dumb Yank tourists. So it fell to her to set off with the shopping list of intravenous accessories. Half an hour later she was pocketing her change as a polite assistant carefully wrapped her purchases.

Some addicts' relationships follow a fairly standard pattern, generally based on one partner being more experienced or motivated in maintaining their habit, with this often developing into more serious controlling behaviour, usually under the guise of protection. Sid and Nancy always seemed to be based much more on equality.

Nancy's needs might have been a driving force in their early days but Sid had caught up in no time, and in many ways overtook her with his voracious intake. The whole picture was to become much more confused once elements like Sid's changing relationship with Johnny Rotten and the group's politics became involved.

By the time we met I'd already had a habit for several years and had learnt a lot about the paradoxical balance between having a good time today while remembering that tomorrow had to be taken care of too. Whenever I was out on a desperate drug search or lay sick, broke and strung out, I'd think back to the times when we'd been awash with gear and using greedily and wish we'd saved some – or surely, out of all that, there must still be a bit somewhere in the flat?

As time went on, the endless sequence of tomorrows – what Burroughs called "the Algebra of Need" – wore me down more and more. Every day I had to perform this ritual, this chemical balancing act, just so that I could pass "Go". As Macbeth said, "And tomorrow and tomorrow and tomorrow". Sometimes the thoughts of years, days, hours, seconds – past and future – became like an obsession, evolving with fractal intensity as the phrase "it's about time" echoed around my head, never meaning the same thing twice. At other times it would all reduce to the simplest bottom line: There's never enough junk in the world to meet all that need or fill all that time.

One afternoon I sat, as so often, on the side of the bath after having a hit. But instead of getting up to smoke a fag as usual, I had a kind of vision, a moment of epiphany. My mind left Camden, Chalk Farm and soared far away from our little basement. Now I contemplated a South East Asian poppy field, endless under a glaring sun and cobalt blue sky. Details gradually became apparent as the picture came more into focus, everything seeming vibrant, intense and super real.

The focus narrowed, homing in on the workers toiling in the field, sweating in the humidity beneath their picturesque conical straw hats. Moving in closer, I could see the raw opium oozing and bleeding from the bulbous poppy heads, black and brown, to be skilfully scraped off with the specially shaped knives evolved especially for the task. Then the next crew took over, ferrying the sticky bales to sheds and warehouses, all bursting with bales waiting to be turned to morphine base and finally into heroin.

The scene flickered and moved on from the production stage to the economic and distribution phases, showing all the financial and social interactions at each stage of the process – a little more corruption seeping out like poison at every stop down the line as the consignment moves further away from its point of origin. Eventually it'll all meld together into a huge bulk shipment, way beyond the power of one man's money to control. All down the line ranks of workers move it on and break it down into kilos, pounds or ounces, until it eventually filters down – much adulterated by then – to the disposable foot soldiers who knock it out in small deals to the rest of the addict army.

Finally I was able to step back and see how the whole process worked like an inverted pyramid, with the field workers at its extended base, then the two sides of the triangle gradually converging until eventually reaching the sharpest point of the apex – the needle going into my arm. I'm not sure the term "end user" even existed then, but I can't think of a much clearer demonstration of the concept than that.

After that I was never able to enjoy the drug or tolerate the lifestyle in the same way. The glass – or whatever other implement – was always half empty from then on. Such doubts and uncertainties didn't trouble Sid and Nancy as they followed the blazing trail to wherever it led. They'd started out like me, just wanting to get as high as possible, to blot out the mundane inanities of routine life, wondering why the rest of the world couldn't just leave them alone. This was no romantic escape into swirling daydreams either – one of the standard put-downs being that addicts can't handle reality (bringing the inevitable rejoinder that "Reality is for people who can't handle drugs") – there's nothing more real than the ticking clock of addiction. Equally, there's often a facile connection made between heroin and sex – usually originating from someone describing the injection rush as "orgasmic" – which doesn't really stand up to analysis if you'll pardon the pun – as Sid discovered, the drug tends to be sexually disabling at first.

For all the intensity of the experiences of heroin and addiction, if I could reach back to those days, my message would be that there are better issues to dedicate your life to than the right to have a heroin habit. Sure, I'd acknowledge that society for the most part is unjust and uncaring – if we thought it was bad back then, look at the world now, torn between rabid capitalists and religious fanatics. If we were guilty of deluding ourselves and over-dramatising our situation, that is as nothing compared to the way that drug addiction is still treated as a criminal matter rather than a medical and social issue. Until that day we'll continue to see lives wasted in punishment and prison, while the bad guys continue to pile up the profits and the law men raise the stakes on their side. Meanwhile the casualties mount up year by year, celebrity and commoner alike.

Thanks

Nina Antonia – Johny Brown– Jo Fender – Vic Godard – Jane Eldridge – Melanie Smith – Hugo Oxley – Phyllis Stein – Inga Tillere – Tony Wilson.